IMAGES
of America

FORTRESSES OF
SAVANNAH
GEORGIA

These officers and NCOs are men of the 48th New York State Volunteer Infantry posing in their dress uniforms on the parapet of Fort Pulaski, Cockspur Island, Georgia. (Collection of Fort Pulaski National Monument.)

IMAGES
of America

FORTRESSES OF
SAVANNAH
GEORGIA

John Walker Guss

ARCADIA

Published by Arcadia Publishing,
an imprint of Tempus Publishing, Inc.
2 Cumberland Street
Charleston, SC 29401

Printed in Great Britain.

Library of Congress Catalog Card Number: 2002108380

For all general information contact Arcadia Publishing at:
Telephone 843-853-2070
Fax 843-853-0044
E-Mail sales@arcadiapublishing.com

For customer service and orders:
Toll-Free 1-888-313-2665

Visit us on the internet at http://www.arcadiapublishing.com

This book is dedicated to Mary Lott Walker, affectionately known to her nephews and nieces as "Aunt Me Nott." Her love and support along with her shared knowledge of history and genealogy has been an inspiration in writing this book.

CONTENTS

Acknowledgments   6

Introduction   7

1.   Establishing a New Colony   9

2.   The British are Coming!   15

3.   Defending a New Nation   33

4.   The Ties are Broken: Prepare for Invasion   39

5.   Building Additional Defenses   73

6.   Defending the Rivers   89

7.   Men Who Stood Upon the Ramparts   113

8.   A New Age of Fortifications   119

Index   127

ACKNOWLEDGMENTS

On May 20, 2001, I came to work for the Coastal Heritage Society in Savannah, Georgia. I had been working in the motion picture industry as an assistant director, but work had been rather slow. A friend, with whom I had worked on the movies *Gettysburg* and *Andersonville,* was managing an old fort down on the Savannah River and asked if I would be interested in joining him. Because of my tremendous love for history and my previous trips to Savannah as a child and a moviemaker, I thought it was a great opportunity to work at a National Historic Landmark.

During my first few months at Old Fort Jackson, while researching the history of the fort and other pieces of Savannah, I noticed there was no collective history on all of these massive fortifications that have guarded Savannah for over 200 years. There was certainly no history of Fort James Jackson. Whether through purpose neglect or oversight, I accepted a personal challenge to write this concise but brief history.

Through a tremendous amount of research, climbing the walls of these forts, and exploring the remains in very unusual locations, I have been able to compile this small archive of the defenses, some still standing and some now brought back into existence only through this book. Through my years of reenacting, I have come to know many of the wonderful people in Savannah who continue tirelessly to preserve these magnificent structures. Special thanks goes to Danny Brown, chief ranger of Fort McAllister State Park; Talley Kirkland, chief historian of Fort Pulaski National Monument; Cullen Chambers, director of the Tybee Lighthouse Museum; Scott Smith, executive director of the Coastal Heritage Society; and my good friends, Marty Liebschner, site manager of Fort James Jackson National Historic Landmark, and Greg Starbuck, previous site manager. Numerous others who have assisted me in my research will be mentioned later in this book.

INTRODUCTION

Gen. James Oglethorpe first came to the new colony of Georgia with great uncertainty as to what was beyond the vast wilderness of this new world. To protect the new citizens of Georgia, one of Oglethorpe's first orders was to construct a fortification around the city to protect the people who would ultimately build this into one of the first 13 colonies of the United States. When the Americans declared their independence from England, they knew there would be retaliation. The only thing they could do is try to prepare themselves for the onslaught of the greatest military power in the world. They had no way of knowing that they would be fighting to take their city back instead of defending it.

After the American Revolution, a new nation began to rise and like any nation around the world, it was important to build fortifications to protect it. President Thomas Jefferson initiated the first orders to construct fortifications along the Atlantic coastline of the United States, which became known as the second system fortifications.

The American Civil War pitted brother against brother, friend against friend, countryman against countryman. When the ties were severed, the South had to prepare itself, much like the colonies had to prepare themselves, for an invasion. Around Savannah, one man who will forever stand in the forefront as one of the most respected military leaders was Robert E. Lee. Lee, a distinguished West Point graduate, came to Savannah in 1829 and returned at the opening shots of the Civil War. His primary mission was to see that important cities like Savannah would be properly defended against Union attack.

As mighty as these brick fortifications were, a new technology was on the horizon. Rifled cannon would prove masonry fortifications obsolete in April 1862, when Union batteries opened fire on Fort Pulaski, located on Cockspur Island. Fort McAllister, located just south of the city, had been built from the earth. It would prove to be more defensible than the once well-engineered brick forts.

In December 1864, man proved to be the ultimate fortification when Gen. William Tecumseh Sherman brought over 60,000 battle-hardened Union soldiers to the front gates of Savannah demanding her surrender. Once the country reunited, new military technology continued to generate and a new system of fortifications was established now on both coastlines of the United States. The Endicott Period became the next phase of fortifications.

World Wars I and II proved that these once magnificent forts were simply works of art and nothing more. The new age of airplanes, mechanized artillery, and ultimately atomic warfare would bring mankind to the realization that there is no literal wall of defense against an enemy.

Fort James Jackson National Historic Landmark, built in 1808, is pictured as it stands today. Named after James Jackson, this fort is Georgia's oldest brick fortification still standing. The Coastal Heritage Society continues to preserve this site after more than 25 years of service.

One

ESTABLISHING A
NEW COLONY

This magnificent monument stands in
Chippewa Square as a memorial to
Gen. James Edward Oglethorpe who, at
the age of 37, set sail with soldiers and
citizens of England for the new land of
America. His party landed in 1733 at the
base of a high plateau along the Savannah
River. It was here that he would build the
majestic city called Savannah. In
establishing this new colony, Oglethorpe first
authorized the construction of a fortification
around the city and outer lying communities
to defend against the natives of this new
world and their adversary, Spain.
(Photograph by John Walker Guss.)

When Oglethorpe began planning the city, he had in mind choosing a strategic position that could be defended in case of attack. He found the perfect site just up river. He wrote to the trustees in London, England, "I went myself to view the Savannah River. I fixed upon a healthy situation about ten miles from the sea. The river here forms a half moon, along the south side of which the banks are almost forty foot high and on top flat, which they call a bluff." Oglethorpe designed this new city with "squares," which were quite beautiful, but could also serve as a defensive position in the event of attack. (Collection of the Coastal Heritage Society.)

In order to defend the southern end of Savannah against possible Native American raids and attacks by the Spanish, who occupied the region of Florida, a fort was built in 1733 by order of General Oglethorpe. It was named in honor of his close friend John, the Duke of Argyle. Today nothing remains of the fort, but this historical marker located on the eastern edge of the Fort Stewart Military Base marks the site. (Photograph by John Walker Guss.)

Built as a wooden stockade fortification, this is the only known sketch of what Fort Argyle may have looked like upon its completion. This palisade style of defense measured approximately 110 feet on each side. It was garrisoned by Captain McPherson with a detachment of Rangers. (Drawing by Bill Drath, Collection of Fort McAllister State Historic Site.)

This palisade wall shows what the fort walls looked like around Fort Argyle as well as most other fortifications built during that period. These reconstructed walls stand at the entrance of Charles Towne, South Carolina's first settlement. (Photograph by John Walker Guss.)

In late 1761, John Gerar William de Brahm, surveyor general of the Southern District of North America, laid out the design for the construction of a fortification on Cockspur Island. It would be named in honor of King George. According to DeBrahm's description, Fort George was a small embrasure redoubt, 100 feet square, with a blockhouse or bastion 40 feet square and 30 feet high. It would serve as a powder magazine, blockhouse, and barracks for up to 50 soldiers. The fort would eventually maintain an armament of 11 cannons and 4 mortars. In 1772, Fort George had been poorly maintained and was considered a total ruin. Only three soldiers and one officer were left to make signals. In 1776, the guns were removed and brought into the fortifications of Savannah to defend against the British. Nothing remains of Fort George. This watercolor was painted in December 1764. (Reproduced from original watercolor by W.J. DeRenne, Collection of John Walker Guss.)

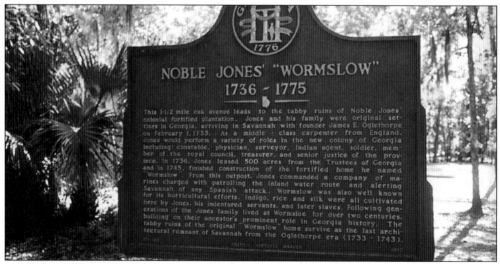

Noble Jones and his family were some of the original settlers of Savannah arriving with James Oglethorpe in 1733. He was a skilled craftsman by trade and proceeded to build a fortified home for his family and fellow settlers. In 1805 the property was virtually abandoned. During the Civil War, earthwork fortifications were built near Wormsloe, which became known as Fort Wimberly. This historical marker stands within the grounds of Wormsloe Plantation. (Photograph by John Walker Guss.)

This is a diagram of the fortified home that Noble Jones completed in 1745. He would name it "Wormslow." Jones had been placed in command of a company of marines to patrol the marsh around his plantation and alert Savannah should any encroaching enemies appear. Today the Georgia Department of Natural Resources has duly preserved what remains of this unique style of fortification. Built of the materials known as tabby, a mixture of sand, shells, and mortar, the Wormsloe home is the only "fortified house" of its kind in the Savannah area. (Collection of Wormsloe State Historic Site.)

This reconstructed home depicts the modest dwellings of many of the new settlers who lived in Savannah and the coastal region. There was one main room downstairs where the daily activities took place such as cooking, eating, and family gatherings. Upstairs was a loft where family members would sleep and it was used for additional storage space. This home is located on the Wormsloe State Historic Site. (Photograph by John Walker Guss.)

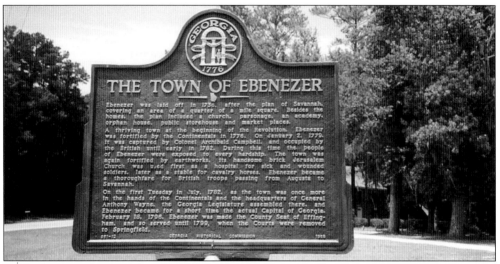

Located just northeast of the town of Rincon stands the small community of what is now called New Ebenezer. Settled in 1736 by German immigrants known as the Salzburgers, the town of Ebenezer was an extension of Oglethorpe's plans to build the new colony of Georgia. The community thrived before the American Revolution, but was ravaged by war—first taken over by Continental troops in 1776 led by Gen. Anthony Wayne. Under the command of Lt. Col. Archibald Campbell, British forces captured Ebenezer from the Americans in 1779. They remained in control until 1782. After the British evacuated the town, General Wayne and his troops returned. In July 1782, the Georgia Legislature assembled here and for a brief time Ebenezer became the capital of Georgia. During the Civil War, Confederate and Union troops marched through Ebenezer leaving behind artifacts that are now on display in the Salzburger Museum next door to the church. (Photograph by John Walker Guss.)

Today the church stands as the only existing structure of the once thriving community of Ebenezer. During the American Revolution, the church was first used as a hospital for sick and wounded British soldiers. It was then used by the British as a place to store supplies and as a stable for their horses during their occupation. Built in 1769, Ebenezer Church is the oldest standing church in the state of Georgia. Worship services continue regularly. (Photograph by John Walker Guss.)

14

Two
THE BRITISH ARE COMING!

As the war became a stalemate in the northern colonies, the British redirected their focus toward the South. Charleston and Savannah were two major port cities and England needed to regain control. Lt. Col. Archibald Campbell led a force southward to Savannah in 1778. He captured the city along with the outer lying townships of Sunbury and Ebenezer.

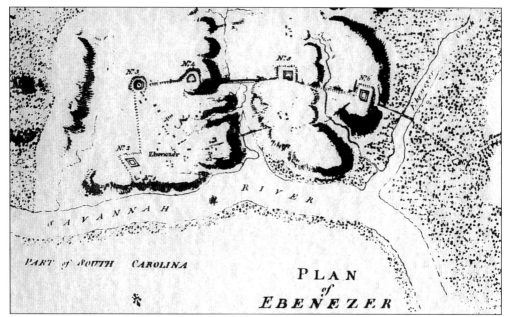

A diagram drawn up by a British officer shows the fortifications around the town of Ebenezer. Six square redoubts or "forts" were built and connected by a series of walls that encircled the town. The redoubts were defended by artillery. (Collection of the Salzburger Museum.)

Ebenezer, located just 25 miles north of the city of Savannah, served as an important part of the outer fortifications guarding the Savannah region. These defenses were strategically built to fortify the town and guard the Savannah River. When the British took over Ebenezer, these fortifications were manned by the 1st and 2nd Battalions of the 71st Regiment of Her Majesty's British troops and 300 men of the Hessian Regiment of Welworth, all under the command of Lt. Col. Archibald Campbell. They were occupied by the British during 1779. Two additional redoubts were built by the British to guard the approach to Zubley's Ferry Road just south of Ebenezer, and one was built on the Ebenezer Creek Causeway to the north of the town. Today Redoubt No. 6 has been well preserved by the citizens of Ebenezer as seen in this photograph. Other portions of the redoubts are preserved as well. (Photograph by John Walker Guss.)

Sunbury was established in 1747 by Capt. Mark Carr who had received land from the President of Georgia. The town grew into a thriving port community exporting many types of goods such as indigo, rice, corn, and timber. Unfortunately, after the American Revolution, the town slowly began to fade due to the expansion westward and the overwhelming competition of Savannah and other new port cities. The only thing that remains of Sunbury is a small cemetery of those who began this new colony called Georgia.

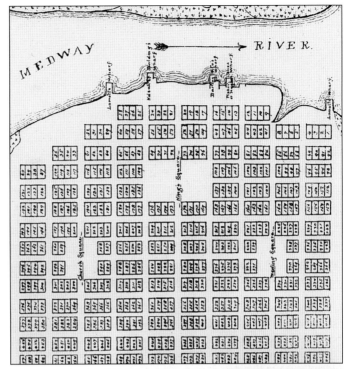

This historical marker designates the site of Fort Morris, named in honor of Captain Morris, who commanded a company of artillery that garrisoned the fort in 1776, just after its completion. Fort Morris standing along the banks of the Midway River was built to defend Sunbury and prevent the British from attacking Savannah from the south. Unfortunately, the fort was captured in 1778 and held by the British until war's end. The well-preserved remains of this earthwork fortification stand just beyond this marker. (Photograph by John Walker Guss.)

On November 25, 1778, Lt. Col. Lewis Fuser had been ordered to take Fort Morris, which was under the command of Col. John McIntosh. Outnumbered more than two to one, McIntosh responded to Fuser's demand for surrender by declaring, "Come and take it!" Uncertain of having adequate forces to take the fort, Fuser retreated to Florida with his force of some 500 British soldiers. Maj. Gen. Augustine Prevost would return with a much stronger force and take the fort the following month. Prevost changed the name to Fort George in honor of King George III. This six-pound cannon, which was used extensively throughout the American Revolution by both British and American troops, stands watch over Fort Morris today. (Photograph by John Walker Guss.)

During the American Revolution, Fort Morris mounted 24 cannons and housed more than 200 soldiers. A large brick barracks stood in the center of the fort. After the war, the fort was reconfigured into a smaller fortification during the War of 1812 and its name was changed to Fort Defiance. During the Civil War, the small earthen fort served as an outpost for Confederate troops. (Photograph by John Walker Guss.)

On December 29, 1778, over 2,500 British troops under the command of Lt. Col. Archibald Campbell landed east of Savannah near Brewton Hill and marched toward the heavily defended American works commanded by Maj. Gen. Robert Howe. The fighting was fierce and the key to the battle came later when a black slave from Sir James Wright's Plantation directed the Light Infantry of Colonel Campbell's command along an unguarded road that flanked the American position on the right. From that point, the battle turned into a route and the Americans were forced to evacuate Savannah. In his journal, Lt. Col. Archibald Campbell wrote, "Gen. Howe and his subordinates, Colonels Eugee and Elbert retreated through the swamp having to leave their horses in the mud. Among the number of American casualties were 83 dead, 38 officers and 415 non-commissioned officers and privates taken prisoner. One stand of colors, 9 brass cannon, 39 pieces of iron ordnance, 23 Cohorns and Mortars, 94 barrels of gunpowder, and a large quantity of arms and stores were captured as well."

Maj. Gen. Archibald Campbell (August 24, 1739–March 31, 1791) of Inverneill, Argyllshire, Scotland, was given charge of eight battalions and sent southward from Sandy Hook, New Jersey, to bring Georgia back under British rule. Campbell captured Savannah from the Americans in 1778 and took Ebenezer the following year. He wasted no time in fortifying these positions, which would ultimately prove impregnable against the American, French, and Haitian advance. Campbell returned to England and served in various positions of military and government affairs. He is buried in Westminster Abbey next to the world-renowned composer, Handel. (Collection of John Walker Guss.)

Gen. Lachlan McIntosh commanded the Georgia Brigade during the first Battle of Savannah. When the British broke through, the order was given by General Howe to evacuate their position. McIntosh and his men were cut off and suffered immense casualties. Lachlan McIntosh (1727–1806) began his military career fighting with Oglethorpe against the Spanish in the Battle of Bloody Marsh. At the outbreak of the Revolution, he was commissioned colonel of the first Continental regiment raised in Georgia. He was later transferred to Valley Forge to serve on General Washington's staff after having been involved in a duel with Georgia signer of the Declaration of Independence Button Gwinnett that resulted in Gwinnett's death. General Washington later described McIntosh as, "an officer of great worth and merit." He continued serving his country until his death in 1806. He is buried with his family in the Colonial Cemetery in Savannah. (Engraving by Hoppner Meyer from a painting by J.B. Longacre after an original portrait.)

Gen. Anthony Wayne (1745–1796) was heavily involved in the campaigns surrounding Georgia. Originally from Waynesboro, Pennsylvania, he was appointed colonel of the Continental troops in Pennsylvania. He served under General Washington, spending the winter at Valley Forge. He was transferred to the Southern theater of operations where he fought in the battles around Savannah. He would later join Washington again in the Siege of Yorktown. Known for his bravery and aggressiveness on the battlefield he was nicknamed "Mad Anthony." He died in Erie, Pennsylvania in 1796. (Collection of John Walker Guss.)

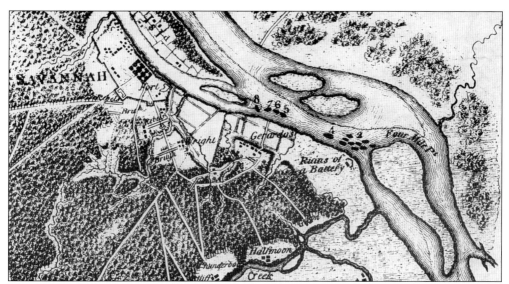

The first fort built on Salter's Island was called "Mud Fort." Made of mud and logs, this earthen battery began construction in 1777 and was manned by Captain Lee's Artillery unit. However, health conditions became so unbearable the fort was abandoned by the time the British fleet even arrived on the Savannah River. Captain Lee died of malaria, which also contributed to the evacuation of the fort. This map, drawn up by a British officer in 1780, shows the defenses about Savannah and mentions the "Ruins of a Battery," which was where the Mud Fort stood. Fort James Jackson would later be built on this site in 1808. (Collection of the Coastal Heritage Society.)

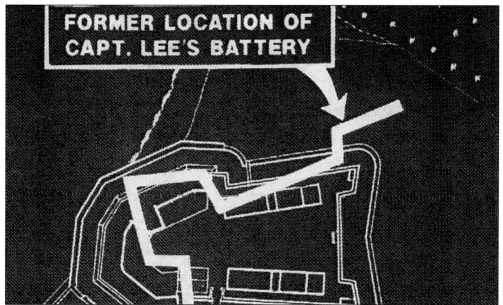

This is a modern drawing taken from an original blueprint showing the outline of Mud Fort. On May 16, 1808, President Thomas Jefferson authorized the purchase of this property from Nichol Turnbull for the sum of $1,800. A brick fort known as Fort Jackson was built on the site where the Mud Fort had once stood. Nothing remains of this first fort built on Salter's Island. (Collection of the Coastal Heritage Society.)

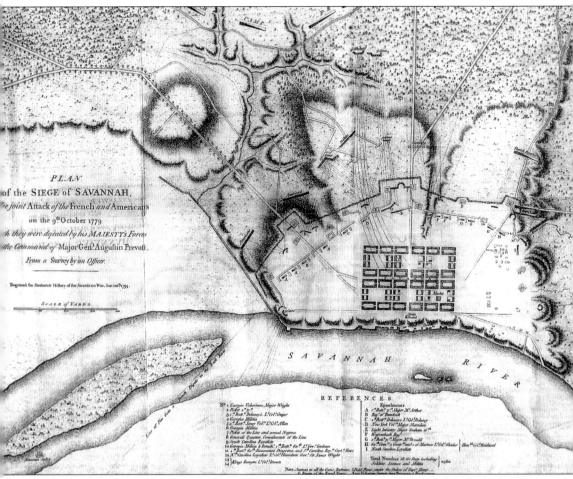

This descriptive map drawn by a British officer displays the siege lines of the American and French forces and the defensive position of the British forces during the Siege of Savannah on October 9, 1779. The Allied forces were superior in number, totaling over 5,000, to the British defenders who numbered some 3,200. However, the British were well entrenched in their fortifications and the Allied command failed to take the initiative in attacking the British before reinforcements their arrived. (Collection of the Coastal Heritage Society.)

Once the scene of some of the most horrific fighting of the Battle of Savannah, this hallowed ground was built upon by the Central of Georgia Railroad in the 1830s. It is documented that the graves of many of the American, French, and Haitian soldiers were desecrated by the railroad during the construction of the Roundhouse complex. Today, the site of where the Spring Hill Redoubt once stood is again in great jeopardy of being built upon. Norfolk Southern Railroad holds the key in their hand as to whether they will honor these American Patriots by handing over this sacred ground to preservationists or wait out for the highest bidder. How can such a price be put on what these men sacrificed?

Located on the southwest side of the city along I-16 this land was deeded by Mordecai Sheftall on August 2, 1773 to be designated as a Jewish Cemetery. During the Battle of Savannah, the cemetery was used as a rallying point for the allied forces as stated in the Orders of the Day of October 8, 1779 by Gen. Benjamin Lincoln. "The second place of rallying on the first if the redoubt should not be carried, will be at the Jew's burying ground, where the reserve will be placed." According to the account of Capt. Antoine-Francoise Tirance O'Connor, a military engineer serving with the French forces on October 9, 1779, shortly after 4 a.m. "The reserve corps, commanded by Vicomte de Noailles, advanced as far as an old Jewish Cemetery, and we placed on its right and a little to the rear the four 4-pounders." (Photograph by John Walker Guss.)

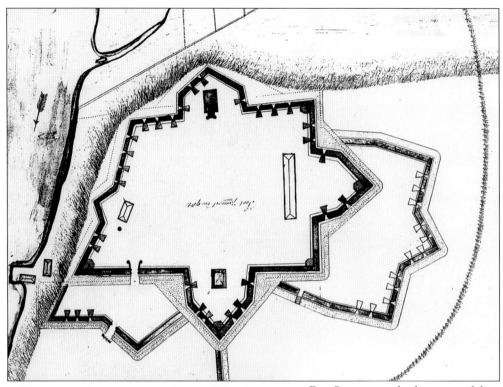

Fort Prevost was built as part of the defenses of Savannah when the British took over the city. Located on the northeast corner of town overlooking the Savannah River, the fort was given its name in honor of their commanding officer, Gen. Augustine Prevost. The fort was redesigned after the war and named Fort Wayne in honor of Gen. Anthony Wayne. Nothing remains of either fort. (Collection of the Coastal Heritage Society.)

Gen. Augustine Prevost, nicknamed "Bullet Head" by his men because of a head wound he had sustained in battle, commanded the victorious British defenders during the Siege of Savannah. He was able to delay the Allied attack long enough to gain reinforcements of Colonel Maitland which may have made the difference in the battle. (Collection of the Coastal Heritage Society.)

Count Charles Henri-Hector Theodat D'Estaing (1729–1794) commanded the overall Allied operations during the Siege of Savannah. He brought more than 4,000 French and Haitian troops to the Georgia coast. Before the attack began, he sent the following demand for surrender to General Prevost: "In the name of the Most Christian Majesty, Louis XVI, you are summoned to surrender your forces." D'Estaing failed to attack immediately after Prevost responded with refusal, which allowed time for British reinforcements to arrive. Having suffered more than 800 casualties, he ordered the withdrawal of French and Haitian troops to the field hospitals at Bonaventure in spite of the insistence from Maj. Gen. Benjamin Lincoln to continue the attack. D'Estaing himself had been wounded twice. Later in life, at the age of 65, he was executed by the guillotine along with Marie Antoinette and others during the upheaval of the French monarchy in the French Revolution. (Collection of John Walker Guss.)

Henri Christophe was just 21 years of age when he joined the French to come to Savannah. Over 550 fellow Haitians joined him in the Battle of Savannah. As the French and American troops were forced to withdraw from the field, the Haitians held their ground covering the retreat. Christophe was among the Haitian soldiers wounded. He returned to Haiti to heal his wounds. Many years later, he became general-in-chief and then king of Haiti in 1811. Unfortunately, just eight years later, the people of Haiti rebelled against him and he committed suicide. (Portrait by Richard Evans c. 1818, Copy Print, Collection of the Coastal Heritage Society.)

Before the American Revolution, Benjamin Lincoln had been a farmer, a town clerk, and a magistrate. He rose to the rank of major general after being promoted by General Washington for his assistance in the defense of New York. Major General Lincoln was transferred South to command the American forces in the Siege of Savannah. He later blamed D'Estaing for the failure of the attack on the British defenses. Lincoln was captured by the British at Charleston and exchanged for General Phillips von Riedesel. Although suffering a miserable defeat at Charleston, he would be given the honor of receiving the British surrender at Yorktown. (Print from an original painting by Chappel, Collection of John Walker Guss.)

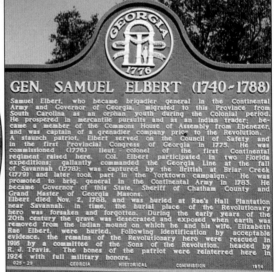

Samuel Elbert was born in 1740 in the Prince William Parish in North Carolina. He moved to Savannah to make a new start for himself after losing his parents at a young age. Before the American Revolution, he became an active member of the Sons of Liberty and joined a militia unit. He rose to the rank of colonel and fought in the losing battle of Savannah in 1778. Elbert was later captured at the Battle of Brier Creek in 1779, but was exchanged in 1781. He rejoined the Continental Army and commanded a brigade at the Siege of Yorktown. After the war, Samuel Elbert served as one of Georgia's governors. Elbert is buried in the Colonial Cemetery in Savannah.

James Jackson joined the American cause as an active member of the Liberty Boys and took part in the raid of the powder magazine in 1775 and the burning of the Rice boats at the Savannah docks. He fought in the Siege of Savannah and was later promoted to the rank of colonel. At the Battle of Cowpens, South Carolina, Jackson distinguished himself by capturing the flag of the 71st British regiment. For his bravery and service throughout the war, General Wayne gave the 26-year-old lieutenant colonel the privilege of receiving the surrender of Savannah on July 11, 1782. After the war, he became heavily involved in politics helping to stamp out the Yazoo Land Fraud. He was a man of great integrity, but had an uncontrollable temper— he was involved in over 20 duels and survived them all. James Jackson was the first Georgian to serve in all three political offices of governor, United States senator, and United States representative. He created the state seal and wrote the first state constitution for Georgia. James Jackson died in 1806 and was buried in the Congressional Cemetery in Washington, D.C. (Collection of John Walker Guss.)

After the disaster of the French and American attack on the British defenses, a Paris newspaper carried this drawing depicting the battle. The brutal fighting that occurred in the city of Savannah would become known as the second bloodiest battle of the American Revolution. Casualties among the Allied troops numbered over 800. As for the British forces, they only suffered 113 casualties. (Collection of Wormsloe State Historic Site.)

Sergeant Jasper's illustrious career began during the Battle of Fort Moultrie in the Charleston Harbor. Through a violent bombardment by the British fleet, Jasper climbed the broken flagstaff and recovered the fallen colors. For his bravery, he was presented a sword by Governor Rutledge and given an officer's commission. He accepted the token, but humbly declined the commission stating he did not feel qualified due to his inability to read or write. During the Siege of Savannah, Sergeant Jasper with his regiment, the 2nd South Carolina, stormed the Spring Hill Redoubt. In an attempt to plant the regiment's colors, he was shot down by British musketry. This 1860 painting depicts Sergeant Jasper's heroic act that immortalized him into history. Sadly, his remains were buried among his fellow patriots in a lost mass grave somewhere west of the city. (Harper's Weekly Newspaper.)

Sgt. William Jasper has become a symbol of American heroism for his bravery during the War for American Independence. For his gallantry, this magnificent statue in his likeness stands in Madison Square. Designed by Alexander Doyle of New York, the cornerstone was laid on October 9, 1879 during the commemoration of the 100th anniversary of the Battle of Savannah. The monument was later unveiled in 1888 and former Confederate General John B. Gordon delivered the address. (Photograph by John Walker Guss.)

He has come to be known as the father of the American Cavalry. Count Casimir Pulaski arrived in America as a result of meeting Benjamin Franklin, who was in search of skilled military leadership. Pulaski, who had been exiled from his native land of Poland, was granted a commission by General Washington. After displaying extraordinary leadership at the Battle of Brandywine in 1777, Washington promoted him to the rank of brigadier general and gave him command of the cavalry. Pulaski raised a cavalry regiment in Maryland that became known as Pulaski's Legion. In 1779, he was ordered south to join General Lincoln in retaking Savannah. During the battle, General Pulaski and his cavalry advanced toward the works of the Spring Hill Redoubt. Through the storm of musketry and cannon fire, he was mortally wounded when grapeshot pierced his inner thigh. He was removed from the battlefield and taken on board the warship *Wasp* where he died. (Collection of Fort Pulaski National Monument.)

This towering monument was built to honor the American hero, Casimir Pulaski. Built in 1854, this elaborate tribute stands in Monterey Square. It was believed at one time that Pulaski's body had been entombed underneath the monument. However, most people agree that when he died on board the warship *Wasp* his body was buried at sea. Towns, schools, parks, and libraries all across the United States have been named in his honor. More significantly, Fort Pulaski was named on his behalf. (Collection of John Walker Guss.)

Gen. James Screven (1750–1778) was another well-known American officer killed in action during the American Revolution. At the age of just 28, he was shot from his horse by British troops during a skirmish at Spencer's Hill around Midway. Several British soldiers then stood upon him firing their muskets into him. He was rushed to Midway Church for treatment and later transferred to a private home where he died. General Screven was brought back to the Midway Church cemetery where he was laid to rest. A fort was built in 1896 on Tybee Island to serve as a defense during the Spanish American War. It had two names until it was named in honor of General Screven. (Collection of the Tybee Historical Society.)

Brig. Gen. Daniel Stewart (1759–1829) served in both the American Revolution and the Indian Wars. Like many military leaders of the time, he established a political career serving in the United States Congress. The active military base in Hinesville, Georgia known as Fort Stewart is named in honor of him. Daniel Stewart is buried beside his wife and children in the Midway Church Cemetery south of Savannah. (Photograph by John Walker Guss.)

This is the monument to Generals Screven and Stewart. Both of these distinguished officers were memorialized with a monument that stands in the center of the Midway Cemetery in the town of Midway. Inscriptions on the monument note their deeds of conduct and heroism. (Photograph by John Walker Guss.)

Maj. Gen. Nathaniel Greene (1742–June 19, 1786) was the most notable general of the Southern Campaigns during the American Revolution. In 1780 he was asked by General Washington to serve as his chief of staff and later given command of all the American Southern forces. Although Greene lost battle after battle to General Cornwallis, he was steadfast in continuing to engage the British army, chipping away at their strength. Ultimately, his persistence had a significant impact on the final battle at Yorktown. After the war, Nathaniel Greene was awarded Mulberry Grove Plantation, 12 miles north of Savannah. Upon his death, he was buried in the Colonial Cemetery. His remains were later reentered to the monument dedicated to him, which stands in Johnson Square. (Collection of John Walker Guss.)

Known to his friends in Savannah as "Gilbert," Marie Joseph Paul Yves Roch Gilbert du Motier, Marquis de Lafayette (1757–1834), was a dear friend of Gen. Nathaniel Greene. They served together with General Washington, and together helped defeat General Cornwallis at Yorktown. After the war, Lafayette visited Savannah on March 19, 1825 to dedicate the monument to his comrade in Johnson Square. He also laid the cornerstone for another fellow soldier, Count Casimir Pulaski, who he had introduced to General Washington. Lafayette stayed in the Owens-Thomas home during his time in Savannah. (Drawn by A. Chappell, Print Copy, Collection of John Walker Guss.)

Three
DEFENDING A
NEW NATION

As a new nation began to grow a need to defend her was of immediate attention. President Thomas Jefferson initiated some of the first brick fortifications to be built by the United States government. One of the first sites chosen in Savannah was Salter's Island where an earthenwork battery had stood during the American Revolution. Additional fortifications would continue to be built long after Jefferson's presidency.

Received on the day of the date of the within written Indenture of the within named Thomas Jefferson President of the United States for the United States, the sum of Eighteen hundred dollars being the Consideration or purchas - money within mentioned to be paid to me

Witness

=W.B.Bulloch

Ben Sheftall Not. Pub.

Nichol Turnbull

Recorded 17 May 1808—

This is a copy of part of the note in which President Thomas Jefferson agreed to pay $1,800 to Nichol Turnbull for the property of Salter's Island for Fort Jackson. The original copy is in the archives of Savannah City Hall. (Collection of Fort James Jackson.)

the Superior Court for Chatham county, the 12th of the present month.

JOB T. BOLLES, *Clerk.*

December 5—145

Wanted immediately,

A journeyman BLACKSMITH. A man who understands his business will have good encouragement and regular employ.

Walter Roe.

December 5—m—145

Wanted immediately,

At Fort Jackson, from fifteen to twenty laborers, who will be allowed 46 cents and a ration per day.

THOMAS BOURKE,

Dec. 5—A—145 *Agent for Fortifications.*

Found,

A sum of money in Bank Notes. The owner may have the same by proving it and paying for this advertisement, and a gratuity to the Negro for his honesty.

December 5—145

Wants a situation,

As Manager or Overseer of a plantation, a YOUNG MAN bred and brought up from infancy to all kinds of cultivation, in the West-

As the new nation began to grow, people were seeking employment. Much like newspapers of today, job opportunities were advertised in the local papers. This ad reads that Fort Jackson is seeking between 15 and 20 laborers to receive 46¢ a day and a ration for assisting in the construction of the fort. (Collection of Fort James Jackson.)

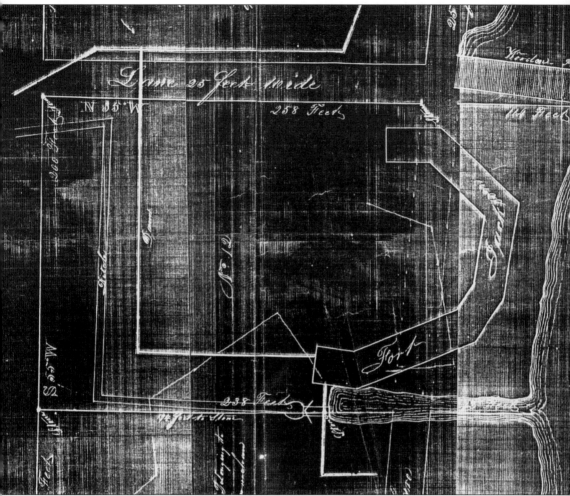

At just 19 years of age, Capt. William McRee (also spelled McRae) was one of only three graduates in the class of 1805. One of his first assignments was to Savannah to Salter's Island to oversee the construction project of Fort Jackson. He later became a colonel in the United States Army and served on the very first United States Army Corp of Engineers board of engineers. These rare blueprints, most likely used by McRee, contain the only evidence of the Mud Fort that existed during the American Revolution. Note the feint outline of the pointed bastion and the extended wall. (Collection of Fort James Jackson.)

Not only were slaves and hired laborers used in constructing forts such as Fort Jackson, but many soldiers were required to pitch in to do whatever it took to build the new line of defenses for America. Secretary of War William Eustis ordered that all West Point cadets "labor or at least be near laborers so as to be able to work if it should be necessary." Soldiers who did work on roads or bridges for 60 days, Sundays not included, received 10¢ extra per day. If they were artificers, they received 14¢ and a "gill of spirits." (Collection of Fort James Jackson.)

There are no photographs known to exist of Fort Jackson upon its completion. However, newspaper sketches were drawn by artists who passed by on board ships. Here, the front of the fort is seen with a dock extended beyond. Supplies were brought in by boat and eventually by train when the rail line from downtown was completed during the Civil War. (Collection of Fort James Jackson.)

This architectural drawing, dated 1823, shows the plan of Fort Jackson along with the plans for the soldier's barracks. The original barracks were constructed of wood and then later improved to becoming brick structures. These barracks remained until December 20, 1864, when, upon their evacuation, the Confederates set fire to the buildings. Only the foundation of the barracks remains today. (Collection of Fort James Jackson.)

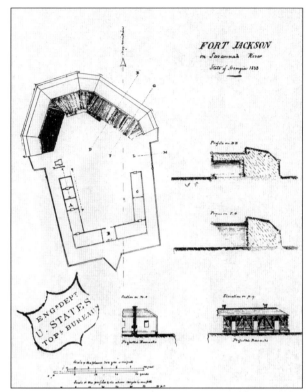

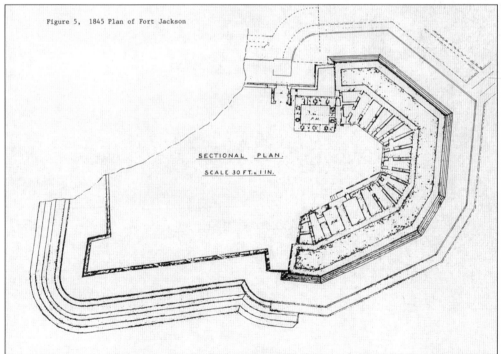

This is a sectional plan of Fort Jackson dated 1845. The drawing shows a detailed design of the parapet and the powder magazine. (Collection of Fort James Jackson.)

Fort Pulaski was named in honor of Revolutionary War hero Casimir Pulaski. Construction began on Cockspur Island where previous forts had been built to provide defense against enemy ships entering the Savannah River, but failed to withstand the test of time. However, this new fort was to be a grand engineering achievement. The fort began its construction in 1829 and was eventually completed in 1847. Some 25 million bricks produced locally were used to build this impregnable fortress. Sandstone and granite were brought from Connecticut and New York as well. As progress continued on the fort, 20 32-pounder naval cannons were mounted in 1840. The fort was designed to carry 150 guns, but no additional cannons were added until Confederate troops seized the fort in 1861. (Collection of Fort Pulaski National Monument.)

Along with Lt. Joseph K.F. Mansfield assigned to the Fort Pulaski project was another officer of West Point. Second Lt. Robert E. Lee, at 23 years of age, was given his first assignment on September 27, 1829 to join the U.S. Army Corps of Engineers on Cockspur Island. There he assisted in the construction of Fort Pulaski. Lee was instructed to oversee the repair of the embankments and drainage systems. He was later promoted to acting assistant commissary of Subsistence of the Post. (Collection of Fort Pulaski National Monument.)

Four

THE TIES ARE BROKEN: PREPARE FOR INVASION

Jefferson Davis (1808–1889) and Abraham Lincoln (1809–1865) were given the daunting challenge of trying to establish and preserve what had developed into two different nations. Jefferson Davis visited Savannah on several occasions during the war and after. Included in his tour was Fort Jackson. However, President Lincoln would never have the pleasure of touring the queen city. The fortifications that had been built to protect the United States became the battlegrounds that would pit American against American. The Civil War brought a new age of warfare, which was the end of these magnificent fortresses.

Savannah, like most cities across the country, saw its streets filled with handsome well-dressed soldiers and jubilant civilians at the beginning of 1861. However, three years later, Savannah witnessed her once jubilant inhabitants fleeing the city in panic when General Sherman and his army pressed the city for its surrender. (Collection of the Coastal Heritage Society.)

The 1st Georgia Volunteers was among the first five regiments authorized by Governor Brown. In this photograph, men of company D stand at parade rest in their dress uniforms. This company, also known as the City Light Guards, was formed in Savannah. The regiment helped in the takeover of Fort Pulaski and remained there throughout the bombardment by Union forces. Many were taken prisoner but returned to service under the Confederate flag. (Copy Print in the Collection of Coastal Heritage Society.)

One of the oldest militia units of Savannah was the Savannah Volunteer Guard. They marched through the streets of the city when Lafayette visited Savannah in 1825. He is reported to have shouted from his balcony, "Ah! Quells beaux soldats!" The Savannah Volunteers would continue to serve throughout the Civil War and both World Wars. When the final call was sounded, the veterans closed the doors to the headquarters on Bull Street that they had known for so many generations. (Collection of the Savannah Volunteer Veterans.)

Another local militia unit known as the Republican Blues served throughout the Civil War. These sketches display the fine uniforms the soldiers wore at the beginning of the war. By war's end, these men and their uniforms would hardly resemble this grand appearance. (Copy Print in the Collection of Coastal Heritage Society.)

This sketch of the Republican Blues made the front cover of *Harper's Weekly* when the men of the unit were in New York City. (Copy Print in the Collection of the Coastal Heritage Society.)

Formed in 1842, the Irish Jasper Greens was another local militia unit that helped in the seizure of Forts Jackson, Pulaski, and all other military installations guarding Savannah. Primarily made up of Irish immigrants, the unit began its service with the Confederacy in garrison at Fort Pulaski and Fort Jackson. Late in the war, the unit was transferred to the operations of Atlanta where it saw heavy fighting that decimated the unit. This soldier's monument in the Catholic Cemetery stands as a symbol of their dedication and sacrifice. Throughout the cemetery, there are numerous graves of Irish who served the United States Army as well as the Confederacy, including the priest who cared for so many soldiers, Father Whelan. Fort Brown, built near this cemetery, was one of the many earthwork defenses during the Civil War. (Photograph by John Walker Guss.)

As soon as the newly mustered Confederate troops seized Fort Pulaski, they quickly raised their new nation's flag. Fort Pulaski was thought to be an impregnable fortress. The Confederates felt secure here. However, it was the calm before the storm of great destruction by the newly invented rifled cannon. (*Harper's Weekly*, Collection of the Coastal Heritage Society.)

The lighthouse on Cockspur Island stood by innocently as Union and Confederate guns roared past her. Built between 1837 and 1839, the beacon amazingly suffered only minor damage during the heavy bombardment of April 10, 1862. It is uncertain as to whether soldiers from either side stood watch from the lighthouse, but it is highly likely. It can only be visited by boat. The Cockspur Lighthouse is part of the Fort Pulaski National Monument. (Collection of Fort Pulaski National Monument.)

The Tybee Lighthouse served as a guard station during the Civil War by both Confederate and Union troops. In November 1861, Confederate troops evacuated the area when the Union fleet was reported in Hilton Head, South Carolina. Upon their evacuation, the Confederates set fire to the lighthouse, destroying the wood interior. When the Union troops moved on to Tybee they repaired the lighthouse and used it as an observation post. (Collection of the Tybee Historical Society.)

This is one of the oldest known photographs of Fort Jackson dating back to 1898. The marshy swamp in the foreground is much the way the ground would have appeared at the time the fort was active. When the state of Georgia began preserving the fort in the 1960s, additional dirt was brought in to keep the fort from washing into the Savannah River. (Collection of Fort James Jackson.)

While stationed in Savannah, Robert E. Lee wrote several letters to his beloved wife Mary describing the work involved in fortifying both Charleston and Savannah against Union attack. On February 23, 1862, he wrote, "His gunboats are pushing up all the creeks and marshes of Savannah, and have attained a position so near the river as to shell the steamers navigating it. None have as yet been struck. I am engaged in constructing a line of defense at Fort Jackson which, if time permits and guns can be obtained, I hope will keep them out. They can bring such overwhelming force in all their movements that it has the effect to demoralize our new troops." Although Fort Pulaski fell early in the war, the Confederates succeeded in maintaining their defenses against the Union until Sherman invaded Georgia. (Letters of Robert E. Lee, Collection of Fort Pulaski National Monument.)

These 32-pounder cannon were part of the armament that guarded Fort Jackson during the war. The full compliment consisted of two 8-inch Columbiads, two 32-pound rifled guns, and three 32-pounder naval guns. Two 12-pounder Mountain Howitzers guarded the rear of the fort in the event of a land attack. (Photograph by John Walker Guss.)

Maj. Edward C. Anderson was a native Savannahian. He had been in the U.S. Navy prior to the Civil War. Anderson was first involved in bringing the ship *Fingal* over from England, which was eventually converted into the CSS *Atlanta* ironclad. He then was given the command of the garrison at Fort Jackson. After the war he became one of Savannah's mayors. (Collection of Fort James Jackson.)

The 22nd Georgia Heavy Artillery mustered in at Griffin, Georgia. They would man the guns of Fort Jackson throughout the war. The regiment detached several of its companies to guard Fort McAllister and other defenses about Savannah as well. These men of the 22nd Georgia Heavy Artillery reenactment unit recreate the life of those men at Fort Jackson regularly. (Photograph by John Walker Guss.)

This sketch in *Harper's Weekly*, dated January 1865, of the rear wall of Fort Jackson depicts a rare view of the barracks and chimneys which once stood inside the fort. The Confederates torched the barracks upon evacuation of the fort on the evening of December 20, 1864. Note the Union ironclads in the immediate background. (*Harper's Weekly*, January 1865, Collection of Fort James Jackson.)

A side view of Fort Jackson shows the impressive engineering of this fort. Although this mighty structure shows signs of deterioration, as seen in the cracks on the corner of the southeastern demi-bastion, Fort Jackson holds firm after nearly 200 years of service. (Photograph by John Walker Guss.)

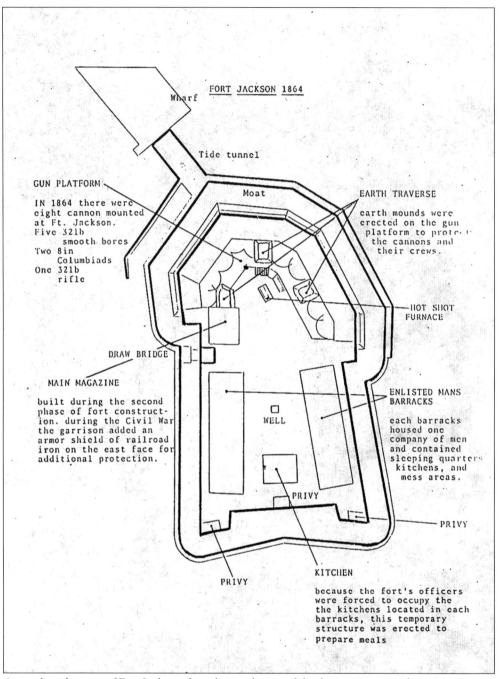

FORT JACKSON 1864

Wharf

Tide tunnel

GUN PLATFORM

IN 1864 there were
eight cannon mounted
at Ft. Jackson.
Five 32lb
        smooth bores
Two 8in
        Columbiads
One 32lb
        rifle

Moat

EARTH TRAVERSE

earth mounds were
erected on the gun
platform to protect
the cannons and
their crews.

HOT SHOT
FURNACE

DRAW BRIDGE

MAIN MAGAZINE

built during the second
phase of fort construct-
ion. during the Civil War
the garrison added an
armor shield of railroad
iron on the east face for
additional protection.

WELL

ENLISTED MANS
BARRACKS

each barracks
housed one
company of men
and contained
sleeping quarters
kitchens, and
mess areas.

PRIVY

PRIVY

KITCHEN

PRIVY

because the fort's officers
were forced to occupy the
the kitchens located in each
barracks, this temporary
structure was erected to
prepare meals

An outline drawing of Fort Jackson describes each part of the fort as it appeared in 1864. During the 1850s many of these additions and repairs had been made to make the fort ready for military service. In the September Annual Report the total cost of renovations was estimated at $50,000. (Collection of Fort James Jackson.)

At 4 a.m. on December 21, 1864, Union soldiers of the 29th Ohio and 28th Pennsylvania entered the fort to find it smoldering from the fires that were set to destroy both barracks and all other materials of military value. (*Harper's Weekly*, Collection of Fort James Jackson.)

This *Harper's Weekly* detailed newspaper sketch depicts Union soldiers on top of the parapet walls of Fort Jackson. The sentry boxes and traverses are the only pieces that don't exist today. (*Harper's Weekly*, Collection of Fort James Jackson.)

William Nutt began his military career with the 55th Massachusetts as a captain in Company D on May 31, 1863. He continued his service and rose to the rank of major. After the Battle of Honey Hill, he went to Hilton Head to arrange for the baggage and stores to join the regiment at Fort Jackson and Fort Bartow. He rejoined the regiment on January 20, 1865. Toward the end of the war, William Nutt became lieutenant colonel of the 55th Massachusetts. He finished the war being mustered out on August 29, 1865. (Collection of the Coastal Heritage Society.)

James Trotter was a schoolteacher before the war. He rose to the rank of sergeant in the 55th Massachusetts and was later promoted to lieutenant on June 11, 1863. He served the remainder of the war and was mustered out on August 29, 1865. (Copy Print, Collection of the Coastal Heritage Society.)

On January 16, 1865, orders were handed down that the 55th Massachusetts be divided among the various forts along the river. Fort Jackson and Battery Lee were garrisoned by Companies C, D, and F and Companies A, B, E, I, and K occupied Fort Bartow located a half mile on the bluff southwest across the rice swamps from Fort Jackson. There, the regiment would have time to mend their wounds sustained on November 30, 1864 in the Battle of Honey Hill, South Carolina. (Collection of the Coastal Heritage Society.)

This view of Fort Jackson was taken in the early 1900s before the fort was abandoned and subjected to neglect and overgrowth. (Collection of Fort James Jackson.)

Once a military post filled with soldiers marching on the parade ground and drilling on the great cannon, Fort Jackson, like so many masonry forts, became obsolete after the bombardment of Fort Pulaski proved that the newly invented rifled cannon could destroy the brick structures thought to be forever impregnable. Through time, Fort Jackson began to disappear among the trees and the encroachment of the Savannah River. New industry also began to threaten the future of the fort's existence. (Collection of Fort James Jackson.)

Fort Jackson was virtually unrecognizable in this photograph taken in 1935. However, the tide tunnel remained distinguishable, as it appears the beacon was still in use to keep ships from running into the fort or aground. (Collection of Fort Pulaski National Monument.)

This photograph taken of Fort Jackson between 1935 and 1940 shows a heavily overgrown east wall. The fort became buried in trees and bushes. There were also few existing records at the time, which made it difficult to determine its significance in history. (Courtesy of Ralston Lattimore-Collection of Fort James Jackson.)

Although marsh grass continues to grow tall throughout the moat in this c. 1935 photograph, the rear walls stand as when they were first constructed. (Collection of Fort James Jackson.)

By 1935, when these photographs of the sally port were taken, the drawbridge had completely rotted away along with the front gates. The first visitors to the fort since its doors had been closed entered an environment that was completely foreign and mysterious. (Collection of Fort Pulaski National Monument.)

In April 1884 the name of the fort was officially changed to Fort Oglethorpe. The fort continued to fall in disrepair and in 1902 all of the fort's armament was removed. Fort Jackson would be overtaken by the overgrowth of trees and underbrush as seen through the doorway of the sally port. (Collection of Fort James Jackson.)

These unidentified men stand in the doorway of the 1870 powder magazine located on the parapet wall. This was a newly designed magazine for the new artillery that would mount the walls of Fort Jackson. However, due to the ineffectiveness of the fort's position as a strong defense smaller cannon were mounted upon its walls. (Collection of Fort James Jackson.)

The main powder magazine had been completed in April 1847. It had lost its roof through neglect and wear. During the Civil War, the roof was covered with iron plating to protect it against incoming shells. Today, the magazine has been restored and houses the fort's theater presentation. (Collection of Fort James Jackson.)

This current view shows the 1847 powder magazine with its reconstructed roof. (Photograph by John Walker Guss.)

Across the yard from the powder magazine is the doorway to one of the many casemate rooms that were used as storage for military supplies. Two rooms are located beyond this doorway. This photograph was taken in 1935. (Collection of Fort Pulaski National Monument.)

AERIAL VIEW of Fort Jackson, Savannah, during the course of limited archaeological excavations, 1968. The fort will soon house the maritime museum of the Georgia Historical Commission. Photo courtesy Robert W. Meiner, Savannah.

In 1965, the Georgia Historical Commission acquired the old fort and decided it was worthy of preservation and creating a museum of maritime history. This photograph, taken in 1968, shows Fort Jackson at last cleared of all underbrush and almost fully restored. A maritime museum was built, a staircase was added, and a periscope exhibit was mounted. (Collection of Fort James Jackson.)

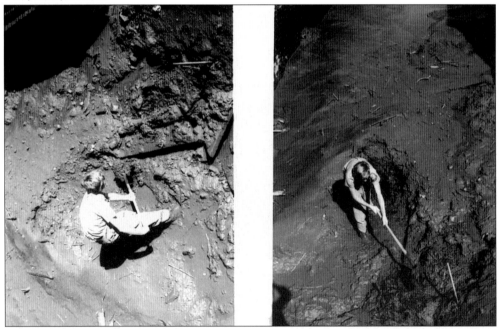

When the Georgia Historical Commission took on the project to resurrect Fort Jackson, much archeological digging took place to recover artifacts in order to learn more about the fort's history. Here a park service official digs in the moat. When the Confederates evacuated the fort, they threw countless numbers of shells, cannon balls, and other military tools into the moat to prevent Union troops from using them. Today many of these artifacts are on display in the fort's museum and at the Savannah History Museum. (Collection of Fort James Jackson.)

Fort James Jackson was a state historic site only for a few years. Because of financial constraints of the state, the fort was once again abandoned. In 1976, a group of concerned local citizens formed a non-profit historic preservation organization that would become known as the Coastal Heritage Society. Their first preservation act was reopening the doors of Fort James Jackson, which would become known as "Old Fort Jackson." (Collection of Fort James Jackson.)

This postcard depicts Fort Jackson as it stood as a state historic site in the 1960s. The fort's museum interpreted the maritime history of the area that included an interesting water mine located in the rear left of this postcard. It has been said the mine was live when it stood as an exhibit piece. The mine was ultimately removed and destroyed. (Photo by Gene Aiken, Collection of John Roberson.)

At the time of these postcards, the history of the fort was obviously in doubt. The back mark states that the fort was built in 1842. (Photo by Gene Aiken-Collection of John Roberson.)

A final aerial look of Fort James Jackson as a National Historic Landmark reveals how close modernization came to nearly overtaking the fort. However, the Coastal Heritage Society, for more than 25 years, has insured the security of this national treasure through its outstanding preservation efforts. (Collection of Fort James Jackson.)

At the outset of the Civil War, Alexander R. Lawton (1818–1896) became the colonel of the 1st Georgia Regulars. On January 3, 1861, one of his first orders was to seize Fort Pulaski. He was quickly promoted to the rank of brigadier general in April 1861 and served as commander of Lawton's Brigade in the Army of Northern Virginia. He was wounded at the Battle of Sharpsburg (Antietam), and upon returning to active duty was appointed as quartermaster general of the Confederacy. One of the earthwork fortifications which stood across from Fort Jackson on the Savannah River was named Fort Lawton in his honor. Toward the end of the war there was a great need for more prison camps. Thousands of Union prisoners of war were sent to the little town of Millen, Georgia where a prison camp had been established called Camp Lawton, also named after the general. (Copy Print, Collection of the Coastal Heritage Society.)

The Lawton family plot overlooks the Wilmington River where during the 1779 Battle of Savannah was the site of where hospitals were set up to receive hundreds of incoming French and American wounded soldiers. This hallowed ground would later serve as a gun emplacement known as the Bonaventure Battery for Confederate cannon guarding the river. (Photograph by John Walker Guss.)

A Martello Tower once stood on Tybee Island during the Civil War and for many years after. This photograph was taken after the Union troops captured Tybee Island and Fort Pulaski. Here, a company of the 48th New York Volunteers stands guard duty in front of this unique style of fortification. Previously, the Confederates fortified the tower with two 32-pound cannons. (Collection of Fort Pulaski National Monument.)

Originally from Savannah, Charles Olmstead (1837–1926) accepted one of the greatest challenges in Savannah at the beginning of the war. His assignment was to defend Fort Pulaski against the Union armies massing against his regiment of the 1st Georgia Regulars. Unfortunately, at that time no one was aware of a new type of rifled cannon that had been produced to annihilate masonry forts. Colonel Olmstead and his men were the first soldiers to confront this new artillery technology. After a severe bombardment, Colonel Olmstead made the difficult decision of turning his sword over to Maj. Charles G. Halpine of the Union Army. Colonel Olmstead and his men were prisoners of war for only a short time and many returned to duty in the Confederate Army. Olmstead went on to serve in Charleston in 1863 and the Atlanta Campaigns of 1864. He was wounded on July 21, 1864 in the fighting around Decatur but returned home to Savannah after war's end. He is buried in Savannah. (Collection of Fort Pulaski National Monument.)

Brig. Gen. Quincy Adam Gilmore will always be remembered as the Union officer who initiated the first successful use of rifled cannons. Until the Civil War, smoothbore cannons were the only proven type of artillery. However, when the Union fleet landed on the Georgia shores, Gilmore convinced Union headquarters that he could take Fort Pulaski by throwing a fierce bombardment at the fort with these new, untested guns. (Collection of Fort Pulaski National Monument.)

Brig. Gen. Quincy A. Gilmore drew his elaborate plans for the siege. Gun batteries were constructed on Tybee Island and across the river on Jones, Turtle, and Dawfuskie Islands in South Carolina. (Collection of Fort McAllister State Historic Site.)

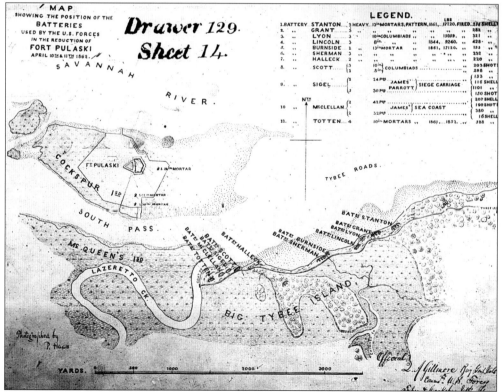

On the morning of April 10, 1862 at about 8 a.m., after commander of the garrison Col. Charles Olmstead refused to surrender Fort Pulaski, the powerful Union guns opened fire. Constant barrages of shells were thrown upon the fort until the next day. By 2 p.m., the southeastern walls had been breached. It was so wide the arches of the casemate were laid bare. A white flag rose from the smoke giving the sign the fort had capitulated. Over 5,000 shells were fired at Fort Pulaski during the bombardment. (Collection of Fort Pulaski National Monument.)

Gaping holes in the seven-foot thick walls of Fort Pulaski proved that masonry forts were no longer a worthy means of fortifying a position. (Collection of Fort Pulaski National Monument.)

One of the precautions the Confederates took in protecting the casemates was to construct heavy slanted wooden walls over the doorways. They dug ditches through the parade ground to keep incoming shells from ricocheting into other areas of the fort. (Collection of Fort Pulaski National Monument.)

This photograph, taken just after the surrender, gives a distinct perspective of how badly the fort's walls were decimated. Had the bombardment continued another day, the fort would have been leveled to the ground. (Collection of Fort Pulaski National Monument.)

Another view of the fort's walls shows the massive destruction. These Union soldiers were very brave to pose in this precarious position inside the fort. (Collection of Fort Pulaski National Monument.)

The once pristine parade ground that both United States and Confederate troops had drilled upon was a total disaster. Confederate troops had dug up the ground and used it to reinforce the timbers they had mounted against the casemate doorways as shown here. (Collection of Fort Pulaski National Monument.)

This Union soldier stands beside a flanking howitzer, which was located in the bastions. These guns defended the drawbridge from an infantry attack in the fort's rear. They stood silent during the bombardment. (Collection of Fort Pulaski National Monument.)

A wide view of Fort Pulaski shows little damage on this side. Once the fort was placed back under the United States government, repairs began immediately on rebuilding the walls and mounting the new rifled cannon. (Collection of Fort Pulaski National Monument.)

The 48th New York State Volunteers, nicknamed Perry's Saints after their beloved Col. James H. Perry, garrisoned Fort Pulaski after the 7th Connecticut served a short period there. These men, mostly from Brooklyn, New York, went on to distinguish themselves honorably serving in many campaigns along the Atlantic coast and suffering the highest number of casualties among all white regiments in the battle of Fort Wagner, South Carolina. Such other battle honors as Olustee, Florida, Bermuda Hundred, Cold Harbor, Drewry's Bluff, and Petersburg, Virginia as well as Fort Fisher, North Carolina would fly upon their colors. (Collection of Fort Pulaski National Monument.)

Baseball had already become a popular game among soldiers both blue and gray. Here, behind the formation of a 48th New York company, is a baseball game in progress. This is the first known wartime photograph of soldiers playing baseball. Abraham J. Palmer, who wrote the History of the 48th New York State Volunteers stated in his unit's history, "Our baseball nine was a fine success…it generally won the laurels. In a game with the 47th New York, played at Fort Pulaski, January 3, 1863, it won 20-7." (History of the 48th New York State Volunteers, Collection of John Walker Guss.)

After Col. James H. Perry unexpectedly died at Fort Pulaski, the leadership was given to Lt. Col. William B. Barton, who had been second the in command of the regiment. He was a strict disciplinarian having come from West Point, but Colonel Barton would prove to be a capable officer, ultimately leading a brigade known as Barton's Brigade. (Collection of Fort Pulaski National Monument.)

Fort Pulaski was never threatened again by Confederate forces. This made it easy for civilians to visit the fort frequently. Here, Colonel Barton and his wife, along with other officers of the 48th New York, pose for a rare photograph. (Collection of Fort Pulaski National Monument.)

Artillery drill was a part of the daily routine of the soldiers at Fort Pulaski. The 3rd Rhode Island Heavy Artillery joined the 48th New York at Fort Pulaski. Together these units trained on the cannon and later cooperated on expeditions through the coastal interior disrupting Confederate operations. Here, the 3rd Rhode Island demonstrates the procedures of loading and firing as this photograph was being taken in 1863. (Collection of Fort Pulaski National Monument.)

This is another angle of the 3rd Rhode Island Heavy Artillery in their drill. Note the dirt and timbers have been removed and the parade ground is filled. (Collection of Fort Pulaski National Monument.)

This gun crew of the 3rd Rhode Island pose for a close-up shot. Their gun was named "Burnside" after General Burnside, a fellow Rhode Islander. (Collection of Fort Pulaski National Monument.)

Outside the front gates of the fort, a city of buildings were constructed to provide housing for additional troops, supplies, ammunition, hospitals, kitchens, livestock, and sutlers. From left to right are Capt. James Farrell, Capt. A. Elmendorf, and Lt. V.R.K. Hilliard. Captain Farrell was killed July 18, 1863 during the assault on Fort Wagner, South Carolina. (Collection of Fort Pulaski National Monument.)

This photograph of the southwest bastion reveals the operations behind the fort. Tons of ammunition were brought in from the Union headquarter and supply base on Hilton Head, South Carolina. From left to right, Capt. L.H. Lent, Powelson, and Lt. S.V.R. Hilliard relax by the gun named "Sprague." (Collection of Fort Pulaski National Monument.)

The officers of the 48th New York State Volunteer Regiment stand together in this one time photograph. The regiment's original commanding officer, Col. James H. Perry, had already died when this photograph was taken. The regiment lost 18 of its officers in combat during the war, which was among the top 10 regiments with the highest number of officers killed in action. (Collection of Fort Pulaski National Monument.)

Five

BUILDING ADDITIONAL DEFENSES

BATTERY LEE AND FORT JACKSON, SAVANNAH RIVER, GA.

If the Confederates were to defend Savannah and prevent Union forces from moving into the interior of Georgia, they would have to build additional fortifications besides the existing masonry forts. Fort Jackson became the headquarters for the Confederate River defenses guarding Savannah. Earthen batteries were built up and down the rivers and were furnished with heavy armament to destroy any ship attempting to sail toward Savannah. This sketch depicts two of the fortifications, Fort Jackson and Battery Lee. Ironclads were later added to stand guard in the river such as the CSS *Georgia* as noted to the far left. Note there were countless numbers of fortified positions built by the Confederates that were unavailable to photograph or retrieve specific information. (Collection of the Coastal Heritage Society.)

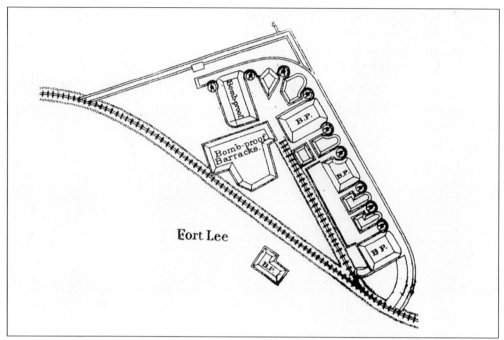

Named in honor of Gen. Robert E. Lee, this outline of Battery Lee, or Fort Lee as it was sometimes called, is one of the few existing diagrams of how the battery was actually laid out. There were nine gun emplacements and six bombproofs with an armament of two 10-inch mortars, two 10-inch Columbiads, one 42-pounder, one 32-pounder Field Piece, and two 24-pounder Howitzers. The battery stood roughly 200 yards down river from Fort Jackson. (Collection of Fort James Jackson.)

Between Fort Jackson and Battery Lee, a railroad track was established to bring supplies and troops to these fortifications from downtown Savannah. (Collection of Fort James Jackson.)

These photographs, taken in 1935 by a National Park Official, show the well-preserved remains of what was once a superbly built earthen fortification. Original plans had been made to incorporate Fort Pulaski, Fort Bartow, Battery Lee, and Fort Jackson into a National Park reservation. However, World War II distracted the attention to historic preservation. After the war, plans changed drastically. Fort Pulaski would be the only fort to be preserved by the federal government. Today many of these mounds have vanished because of the encroachment of the river and the failure of a local corporation to donate the site to local preservationists. (Collection of Fort Pulaski National Monument.)

This photograph of Battery Lee shows that at one time the earthwork was clear cut to make it accessible.(Collection of Fort Pulaski National Monument.)

This is an excellent view among the bombproofs. Again, the area appears to have been cleared for preservation efforts. (Collection of Fort Pulaski National Monument.)

In April 2002, these rare photographs were taken of the final remains of the gun platforms and the railroad planks of Battery Lee. They are perhaps the only existing gun platforms that remain among all of the fortifications built around Savannah during the Civil War. However, they will suffer the same fate unless historic preservationists and the present corporation of Kerr McGee, who owns the site on which the fort stands, can work together to save this historic site. Time is running out. (Photograph by John Walker Guss.)

These large wooden platforms were put together with large wooden pegs, which amazingly have withstood over 140 years of the crashing wakes and large pollutants of the Savannah River. (Photograph by John Walker Guss.)

Wooden planks were driven into the sand to build the foundation for the rail line built over them. During the war, troops and ammunition were continuously carried along these tracks. (Photograph by John Walker Guss.)

A closer view of these gun platforms shows how well they must have been constructed to be preserved all these years. On these planks stood cannons that weighed some 7,000 to 9,000 pounds. (Photograph by John Walker Guss.)

For years Fort Jackson and Battery Lee stood together along the Savannah River. However, large corporations began to build along the waterfront, destroying the serene view one could have standing atop the ramparts. Another gun platform stands in the foreground just yards away. (Photograph by John Walker Guss.)

One of the largest earthen fortifications guarding Savannah was named in honor of Brig. Gen. William Robertson Boggs (March 18, 1829–1913). Born in Augusta, Georgia, Boggs was a graduate of West Point and became a topographical engineer in the Corps after graduation. When the Civil War began, he came home to serve as an officer in the Confederate Corps of Engineers. He was sent to Charleston, South Carolina to serve under General Beauregard. He was later promoted to chief engineer of Georgia in 1862. There he helped devise an intricate system of earthen fortifications surrounding Savannah. After the war, he became a professor at Virginia Polytechnic Institute (now VMI.) He died at his home in Winston-Salem, North Carolina. (Collection of the Coastal Heritage Society.)

Fortifications that became known as Fort Boggs were constructed approximately two miles east of the city. Local plantation owners released their slaves to the military in order to assist in the building of these defenses. This news reporter noted that, as the slaves worked, they carried on a song or ditty. (The *Illustrated London Newspaper* April 18, 1863, Collection of John Walker Guss.)

Slaves from Georgia and South Carolina helped build the defenses all about the Savannah area. This detailed newspaper sketch demonstrates the technique of piling up the sand and then pounding it to compress and stabilize the mounds in what would become a formidable defense. (The *Illustrated London Newspaper* April 18, 1863, Collection of John Walker Guss.)

Fort Boggs was never challenged by water or land, but it was considered by one Confederate officer to be "one of the finest field works constructed on either side during the war." It was constructed in a five-point configuration with batteries extending southward.

Very little remains of the magnificent fortifications constructed by these slaves. Today, where Fort Boggs once stood is now the Savannah Golf Club golf course on President Street. Some of the works remain as a testimony to the men who built them and defended them. (Collection of John Walker Guss.)

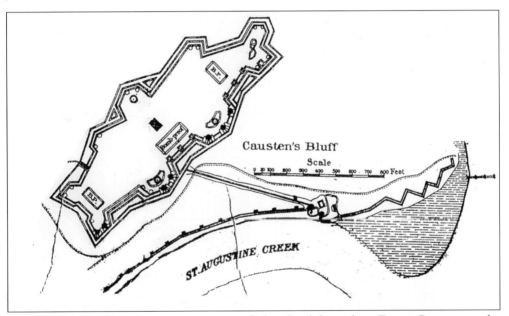

Causton's Bluff, or Fort Bartow as it was named after Confederate hero Francis Bartow, was the largest of all the enclosed earthen fortifications guarding Savannah. The fort had an armament of one 10-inch Columbiad, two 8-inch naval guns, two 8-inch Columbiads, two 24-pounder and one 12-pound rifled cannons, two 8-pounder Smoothbore guns, two 6-inch and three 3-inch rifled guns, and one Boat Howitzer. Another battery in front of Fort Bartow maintained two 32-pounder smooth bore cannons.

These pictures of Causton's Bluff, on which Fort Bartow once stood, are part of the series of the 1935 survey taken by the National Park Service photographer. Fort Bartow, which guarded St. Augustine Creek, was part of the interior line of defenses running along the smaller rivers and creeks surrounding Savannah. This string of earthworks was anchored on the left by Fort Bartow and ran all the way south to the batteries on Rose Dew Island. (Collection of Fort Pulaski National Monument.)

Through the years, the fort surrendered to the development of residential neighborhoods. Many of these hand-forged earthworks continue to be bulldozed to make way for new multimillion-dollar homes. This once grand fort is known only in the name of the gated community, Causton's Bluff.

At the beginning of the war, the Confederates tested new types of cannons. While visiting Fort Bartow, Gen. Robert E. Lee witnessed a trial of a new cannon. The gun experienced problems and exploded in half with one half nearly killing the general. Half of the cannon was recovered in 2000 by the staff of Fort Jackson and is currently being preserved at Fort Jackson National Historic Landmark. (Photograph by John Walker Guss.)

At the beginning of the war, many of the newly constructed defenses throughout the Confederacy were poorly equipped with these new volunteer troops, as Lafayette McLaws pointed out in a letter to his wife on April 26, 1861. He wrote, "I am now the commanding officer of Thunderbolt Point, a place on San Augustine Creek, about five miles from the city-I went there this morning and found three companies of the Volunteer force viz. The Cherokee Brown Riflemen (2nd Georgia Infantry Co. F.) under the command of Captain Dickerson, Wrights Infantry (2nd Georgia Infantry Co. H.) under Captain Glenn, and Buena Vista Guards (2nd Georgia Infantry Co. I.) under Captain Butt (Later Colonel.) and not one had cartridges. Wrights Infantry and the Buena Vista Guards had no arms, accoutrements or ammunition-and the Buena Vista Guards had no tents." (*Harper's Weekly*, Collection of John Walker Guss.)

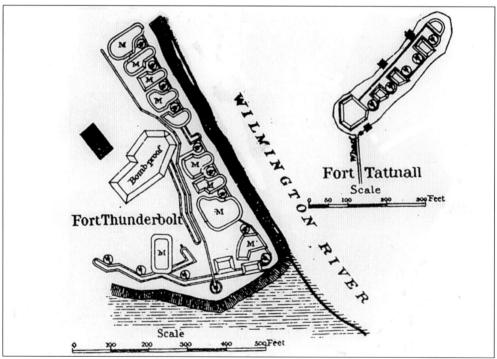

The battery built on Thunderbolt Island was situated along the Wilmington River, which was a back entrance to Savannah. Batteries Tattnall and Lawton stood across from Fort Jackson and Battery Lee guarding the primary focus of the Union forces, the Savannah River. (Collection of Fort McAlister State Historic Site.)

Thunderbolt Battery maintained an enormous arsenal of one 10-inch Columbiad, two 8-inch Columbiads, two 8-inch shell guns, one 42-pounder rifle gun, one 42-pounder smoothbore, and six 32-pound field guns. (*Harper's Weekly*, Collection of the Coastal Heritage Society.)

When the men were not on duty they relaxed on the walls of the fort. Some enjoyed a bit of fishing. (*Harper's Weekly*, Collection of the Coastal Heritage Society.)

Beaulieu Battery, located at the junction of the Burnside and Vernon Rivers, was supported by one 8-inch Columbiad, two 10-inch Columbiads, two 24-pounder guns, and three 32-pounder field guns. To the southwest guarding the Little Ogeechee River was Battery Rose Dew. (*Harper's Weekly*, Collection of Fort McAllister State Historic Site.)

Fort McAllister was built to the south along the Ogeechee River. It stood alone as part of the land defenses but had the company of the CSS *Nashville* until the ship was destroyed by Union ironclads. (Collection of Fort McAllister State Historic Site.)

Battery Stephens on Green Island added to the defenses of Savannah. However, due to its isolated position from the other fortifications, it was abandoned at the beginning of the war. The powder magazine is in excellent condition as seen in these photographs taken in May 2002. Green Island is not accessible by boat and Battery Stephens stands on private property.

Among the batteries on the Isle of Hope were Battery Daniels, Fort Wimberly, and Battery Beaulieu, which guarded the entrances to the Vernon and Burnside Rivers. Pews of this nearby Methodist Church built in 1859 were used as beds for the sick and wounded. Today 33 Confederate soldiers of Effingham County are buried in the front courtyard of the church. (Photograph by John Walker Guss.)

Six

DEFENDING
THE RIVERS

Commodore Josiah Tattnall (1795–1871) was 66 years old at the time of the Civil War. He had served as a midshipman in the United States Navy just before the War of 1812. In 1859, he was engaged in an Anglo-French naval attack against Chinese fortifications. He broke American neutrality and later stated, "Blood is thicker than water." When the Civil War erupted, Tattnall was placed in command of the Confederate Naval forces around Savannah. His small fleet became known as the "Mosquito Fleet." Josiah Tattnall was born and raised in Savannah. He was buried among his family in Bonaventure Cemetery, which had once been his family's plantation. He will always be remembered for his outstanding devotion to duty and his extraordinary leadership. A fellow naval officer wrote years later, "He possessed all the traits which are found in heroic characters, and with suitable opportunities, would have set his name among the great naval worthies who are historic." (Photograph by John Walker Guss.)

Henry F. Willink Jr. operated a shipyard in Savannah. In November 1861, the Confederate Navy Department contracted him to build the new age of naval warfare. The CSS *Atlanta*, CSS *Savannah*, and the CSS *Georgia* were all built in Savannah. Later the CSS *Milledgeville* and CSS *Macon* would become works in progress, but would never touch the Savannah River. (Collection of Fort James Jackson.)

Capt. W.A. Webb was assigned to the new ironclad CSS *Atlanta*, which would help defend the rivers around Savannah. Unfortunately, the entire crew would be captured in June 1863 and sent to Fort Warren, Massachusetts, as prisoners of war. (Collection of Fort James Jackson.)

Crew of the Confederate States Ironclad "Atlanta" in prison - Fort Warren, Boston Harbor, Mass. 1863

The CSS *Atlanta* was built from a converted ship, the *Fingal*, which had originated from the Scottish shipyards of J&G Thomson. It sailed from Europe to Savannah at the beginning of the war and was trapped upon its arrival by the Union blockade. She was cut down and redesigned with three layers of oak and pine planks, and rearmed with four-inch-thick iron plating. Stretching 204 feet in length she carried four rifled guns and a spar with a percussion torpedo attached at its stem, much like the submarine CSS *Hunley*. The *Atlanta* attempted to break the blockade in June 1863, but was confronted by several Union warships, including the USS *Weehawken*. The *Atlanta* ran aground and was forced to submit. (Collection of the Coastal Heritage Society.)

After the capture of the CSS *Atlanta*, she was sent north for repairs and restructuring. She then served on the James River in Virginia. (Collection of the Coastal Heritage Society.)

For Southerners this was not a pleasing sight. The new officers of the now USS *Atlanta* pose for a photograph. (Collection of the Coastal Heritage Society.)

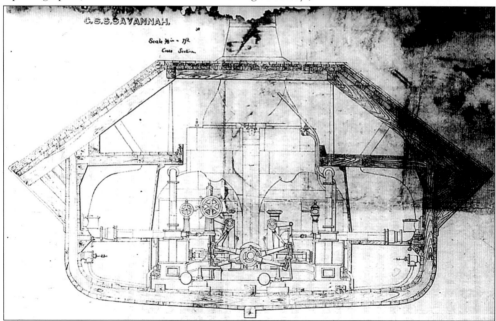

Few blueprints exist of the Confederacy's fleet of ironclads. This partial blueprint of the CSS *Savannah* is a rare document of the ironclads built by the Confederacy. (Collection of the National Civil War Naval Museum.)

The CSS *Savannah* was built at the local shipyards and helped keep the Union fleet at bay throughout its service. Early in the morning of December 21, 1864, as Confederate forces crossed over into South Carolina, remaining troops blew up the *Savannah* in the river. The following day, when General Sherman arrived in Savannah, he climbed to the top of the City Exchange and surveyed the river and surrounding area. Just east of downtown he witnessed the charred skeletal remains of the CSS *Savannah*. (*Harper's Weekly*, Collection of the Coastal Heritage Society.)

Sometimes known as "The Ladies Gunboat," "The Ironclad Battery," and numerous other nicknames, the CSS *Georgia* was launched in 1862. The ladies of Savannah and other major cities of Georgia formed the Ladies Gunboat Association and raised $155,408 to have this ironclad ship built in Savannah. The massive ship stretched over 150 feet in length and over 50 feet wide. It mounted an arsenal of 10 cannon. The *Georgia* joined the rest of the naval ships in protecting the Savannah River. Although it fought in no engagements, it proved to be a serious threat to any Union vessel trying to sail up the river. The propulsion system was so poor on this massively heavy ship that it had to be maneuvered up and down the Savannah River by tugboats and the engines had to run constantly so the ship would not sink. Upon the evacuation of the Confederate forces from Savannah on the evening of December 20, 1864, the ship was scuttled in front of Fort Jackson and rests there today some 40 feet on the river floor. (Collection of the Coastal Heritage Society.)

The CSS *Georgia* was heavily armed with cannons and well protected with armored plating. One reporter from a Northern newspaper wrote, "She is armed with 12 cannon and plated with railroad iron." This cannon along with numerous Brooke Rifle Shells and some of the armor plating were raised from the *Georgia* during an archeological dive conducted by the University of Texas A&M and the United States Army Corps of Engineers in 1986. These artifacts are on display at Fort James Jackson in Savannah. (Photograph by John Walker Guss.)

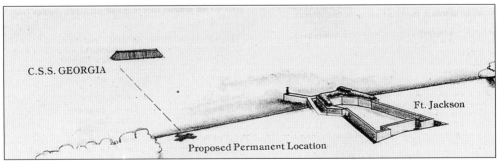

C.S.S. GEORGIA

Ft. Jackson

Proposed Permanent Location

When the Confederate garrison evacuated Fort Jackson, the navy scuttled the *Georgia* to the bottom of the river. In May 2002, new sonar devices were used to detect the exact position and condition of the ship. Those results are still waiting to be determined. A second archeological dive is being planned by the United States Army Corps of Engineers for the fall of 2002 to determine specifically what remains of the *Georgia* and the future of one of the few remaining, if not the only, Civil War ironclad in existence. (Collection of the Coastal Heritage Society.)

One of the few bright moments for the Confederate Navy on the Savannah River was the night capture of the USS *Waterwitch* on the Ossabaw Sound on June 3, 1864. In a report to Secretary of the Confederate Navy S.R. Mallory, William Hunter, flag officer of the Savannah Squadron, sent the flag of the *Waterwitch* to Richmond as a trophy. (Collection of the Coastal Heritage Society.)

In addition to the death of the commanding officer of the mission, Lt. Thomas P. Pelot, were Moses Dallas, an African American serving as the pilot for the Confederate expedition, and fireman William Crosby. He along with the others were buried in Laurel Grove Cemetery. (Photograph by John Walker Guss.)

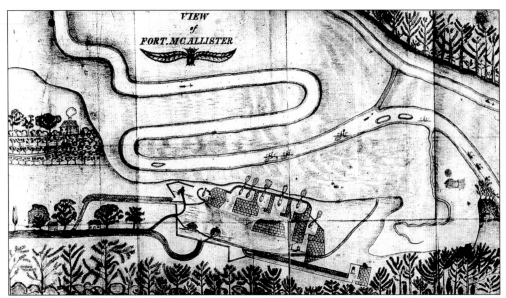

Fort McAllister, built as an enclosed earthwork fortification to guard the Ogeechee River entrance, was the only fort in all of the Savannah defenses to be engaged in an all-out, hand-to-hand battle between the Confederate garrison and the 14th Corps of the Union Army. (Collection of Fort McAllister State Historic Site.)

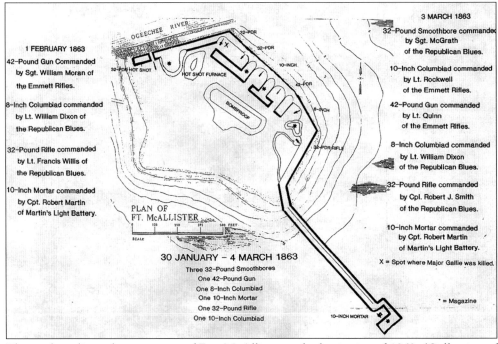

This outline shows the armament of Fort McAllister at the beginning of 1863. (Collection of Fort McAllister State Historic Site.)

96

Originally from Charleston, Capt. John McCrady engineered this earthwork fort originally known as the Genesis Point Battery. It would later be called Fort McAllister after the man responsible for donating the property, Joseph McAllister. (Collection of Fort McAllister State Historic Site.)

After the commanding officer, Major Gallie, had his head blown off by an incoming shell, the leadership was passed to his second in command, Maj. George W. Anderson Jr. He commanded the besieged garrison of Fort McAllister. Anderson noted, "It was evident, cut off from all support, and with no possible hope of reinforcements from any quarter, that holding the fort was simply a question of time." The assault commenced on December 13, 1864. (Collection of Fort McAllister State Historic Site.)

Dougald Ferguson (May 7, 1838–March 7, 1892) joined the Republican Blues just before the Civil War. Here he poses for a photograph in his dress uniform for which the Republican Blues was noted. Ferguson and his comrades helped defend Savannah, which included Fort McAllister. He survived the war and lived until 1892. He is buried in Lot #196 in Laurel Grove Cemetery. (Collection of the Ferguson and Seyle Families of Chatham County.)

Pvt. Elbert C. Sims enlisted in Company K of the 7th Georgia Cavalry on April 1, 1862. This regiment, which came out of Bryan County, was nicknamed the "Hardwicke Rifles" and was commanded by Capt. Joseph Longworth McAllister. Sims and his regiment spent much of the war guarding the Georgia coast stationed at Fort McAllister. Later they were transferred to Virginia. On December 6, 1864, Sims was captured while he was at home on furlough and was sent to Point Lookout prison where he died of pneumonia on February 17, 1865. (Fort McAllister State Historic Site.)

Numerous attacks were made on Fort McAllister by Union ironclads and gunboats. However, they could never pound the stubborn fort into submission. Earthwork fortifications were easy to restore after a bombardment because the dirt walls could easily be rebuilt after an attack. It is interesting to note that the artist drew a cannon ball flying through the marsh. Perhaps he actually witnessed this. (Collection of Fort McAllister State Historic Site.)

Ironclads were the only ships the Union had that had any hope of breaking through the Ogeechee River against the guns of Fort McAllister. On March 5, 1863, the ironclads *Patapsco*, *Passaic*, and *Nahant* made another of many attempts, but failed. (Collection of Fort McAllister State Historic Site.)

Both navies battled back and forth through the rivers around Savannah. The CSS *Nashville* was successful in terrorizing the Union Navy at the beginning of the war. However, on February 28, 1863, the USS *Montauk* engaged the CSS *Nashville* in a fierce battle that resulted in the destruction of the Nashville. To no avail, the guns from Fort McAllister could not aid the

Nashville before she was destroyed. The remains of the ship rest at the bottom of the Ogeechee River in front of Fort McAllister. Artifacts are on display at Fort McAllister State Historic Site. (The Soldier in Our Civil War, Collection of John Walker Guss.)

In December 1864, when General Sherman's army approached the outskirts of Savannah, he detached 34-year-old Gen. William B. Hazen with over 5,000 troops of the 14th Corps to capture Fort McAllister in order to open the lines of communication between the Union Navy and the Union Army. The small garrison of just 150 Confederates could not withstand such an attack. In just a matter minutes Hazen's troops overran the fort. Among the Confederate casualties there was a total of 16 killed and 28 wounded. In addition were 2nd Lieutenant Hazzard, who was killed; 1st Lieutenant Schirm, who was shot in the head; and Captain Morrison, who was shot through both legs. Capt. N.B. Clinch suffered 11 wounds. (Collection of Fort McAllister State Historic Site.)

This was the view the Union troops had during their assault on Fort McAllister. Abatis, which consisted of logs and brush, was piled around the fort to slow down attacking infantry. In this case it did little to stop the overwhelming Union onslaught. (Collection of Fort McAllister State Historic Site.)

After the capture, Northern photographers took numerous photographs of Fort McAllister. This particular shot shows the deep gorge the Union troops had to cross, then pass through the wooden palisades, and up over the walls. It is said the attack lasted just 15 minutes. Note the size of the soldier compared to the deep gorge. (Collection of Fort McAllister State Historic Site.)

Once Fort McAllister was silenced, her cannons were repaired and put back into position for action like this 32-pounder. (Collection of Fort McAllister State Historic Site.)

Fort McAllister kept a vigilant watch over the Ogeechee River throughout the war. Here one can see westward from the fort. The Union soldier is sweeping the deck of the gun platform. The steamship in the background is blurry because photography of that time could not take clear photographs of moving objects. (Collection of Fort McAllister State Historic Site.)

This was the view the Confederates had when the Union legions approached and surrounded Fort McAllister. It was, in some respects, the same perspective the defenders of the Alamo faced against Gen. Santa Anna's Mexican forces. However, the Union army did not slaughter the defenders. Looking westward, the Union encampment with its tents and bustling campfires can be seen in the distant. (Collection of Fort McAllister State Historic Site.)

This is an excellent example of a cannon being placed on its carriage with the use of the pulley system. These Union soldiers have just mounted a Columbiad cannon. (Collection of Fort McAllister State Historic Site.)

Once repairs had been made on the fort and the landmines were removed throughout the outer works, Fort McAllister became a quiet place for its new residents. (Collection of Fort McAllister State Historic Site.)

The distinguished General P.G.T. Beauregard had served in many of the major campaigns during the war. He was ordered back to Charleston to oversee the coastal defenses. He would give General Hardee the final order to abandon Savannah. In one of his final dispatches, dated December 15, 1864, Beauregard wrote, "Under no circumstances must you be cut off from junction of your forces with those of General Jones. The safety of Georgia and South Carolina depends upon the result." (Collection of Fort James Jackson.)

Gen. William Hardee, a former West Point graduate and the author of the widely used *Hardee's Infantry Drill Manual*, was faced with the difficult task of trying to defend a helpless position. He had less than 10,000 able-bodied combatants scattered over a massive front against General Sherman's overwhelming force of 60,000 infantry and nearly 5,000 cavalry. Ultimately, Hardee ordered the evacuation on the evening of December 20, 1864 of all soldiers and civilians who could move into South Carolina. (Collection of Fort McAllister State Historic Site.)

Gen. William Tecumseh Sherman led over 60,000 Union soldiers from Atlanta to Savannah. However, the journey had originally begun as far north as Chattanooga, Tennessee. He became one of the greatest generals in United States history, but also one of the most despised of all Union generals for waging war against the entire Southern civilian population. (Collection of Fort McAllister State Historic Site.)

The CSS *Georgia*, along with numerous other ships, was constructed at the shipyards located where the Marriott Hotel stands today. On the eve of December 20, 1864, Confederates put the torch to these shipyards to keep them out of the hands of the Union army. The ironclad *Milledgeville*, which was still under construction along with another ironclad and the tugboats *Firefly* and *Isondigo*, would never be launched into the Savannah River. (Frank Leslie's Illustrated-Collection of John Walker Guss.)

These types of wooden pontoon bridges were hastily built across the Savannah River (along River Street) in order to help evacuate all Confederate military personnel and civilians.

Sgt. W.H. Andrews described the following in his memoirs:

"Tuesday night, December 20, 1864, the forces of Gen. Hardee evacuated the city of Savannah, Ga. The Regulars (1st Georgia Regulars) were withdrawn from the works about eleven o'clock, and I will never forget passing through the city which was sealed. Doors were being knocked down, guns firing in every direction, the bullets flying over and around us. Women and children screaming and rushing in every direction. All combined made it a night to never be forgotten by them who witnessed it. We finally reached the river where a string of rice barges strung end to end formed a bridge for us to cross on. The bridge was a poor makeshift, but the army succeeded in crossing it. While crossing the bridge, our way was lighted up by the burning of the Confederate gunboats (C.S.S. Georgia and C.S.S. Savannah.) and other vessels lying in the Savannah River. Sad to look at, but at the same time made a beautiful picture on the water. After the army had crossed, the barges were cut loose and destroyed."

(Sketch from *Harpers Weekly* from the Collection of the Coastal Heritage Society, Text from *Footprints of a Regiment Memoirs of 1st Sergeant W.H. Andrews.*)

On December 20, 1864, General Hardee sent out Confidential Circular No. 2 which provided the order of the evacuation. Wright's division would move at 8 p.m., McLaw's division at 10 p.m., and Smith's division at 11 p.m. Skirmishes of each division would retreat thereafter. Once the Confederate forces successfully crossed over into South Carolina, they marched toward Hardeeville where all Confederate forces converged and then moved northward to prepare for Sherman's advance. (Collection of the Coastal Heritage Society.)

On December 22, 1864, General Sherman and his army rode in to the streets of Savannah. He wrote in a telegram to President Abraham Lincoln, "I beg to present to you, as a Christmas gift, the city of Savannah, with 150 heavy guns and plenty of ammunition, and also about 25,000 bales of cotton." Between November 16 and December 10, the Union army had marched some 255 miles from Atlanta to Savannah. (*Harper's Weekly*, collection of John Walker Guss.)

In addition to the gun batteries along the river, large pilings were driven into the river's floor to create a barrier to keep Union ships from coming up river. There were also torpedoes and mines placed in the water. Once the Confederates evacuated their defenses, Union troops were able to dismantle the obstructions which had kept them out for nearly the entire war. (Collection of the Coastal Heritage Society.)

When the Confederates evacuated their works, the Union army moved in and raised the American flag. In addition to the earthworks, the marsh had formidable defense in itself. (*Harper's Weekly*, Collection of the Coastal Heritage Society.)

Built in 1838, the Central of Georgia Railroad played a very important role throughout the war, not only for Savannah but for the rest of the Confederacy. The shops at the Roundhouse built war materials, which included the doors and gun carriages of Fort Jackson. As Sherman marched through Georgia, Union prisoners of war were dispersed throughout the state by railroad from Andersonville to other prisons, which included Millen, Blackshear, and Savannah. After the war, travelers like Robert E. Lee and Jefferson Davis revisited the city by rail. (Photograph by John Walker Guss.)

Sherman's men cleared a path of destruction across the state of Georgia, then through the Carolinas. One of the most important military strategies was destroying the lines of communication and transportation. Hundreds of miles of track were torn up, burned, and then wrapped around trees to render them useless to repair. The Central of Georgia was crippled severely.

This was the Union Army staff, who devised the plans of conquering the South. From left to right are Maj. Gen. O.O. Howard, Maj. Gen. John A. Logan, Gen. William B. Hazen, Maj. Gen. William Tecumseh Sherman, Maj. Gen. Jefferson C. Davis, Maj. Gen. Henry W. Slocum, J.A. Mower, and Maj. Gen. Francis Preston Blair Jr. (Collection of Fort McAllister State Historic Site.)

Seven

MEN WHO STOOD UPON THE RAMPARTS

From the beginning until the end of the Civil War, thousands of soldiers both blue and gray passed through the gates of Savannah. Miles and miles of earthen fortifications were built by these men whether they were under siege or on the offensive. However, this monument only honors the men of the Confederacy and their bravery in defending Savannah and Georgia. This magnificent Confederate Monument was sponsored by the Ladies Memorial Association and placed in the heart of the city in Forsyth Park in 1874. The monument was designed by Robert Reid and built in Canada. Sentiments were still strong against the North after the war—so much that the monument was put on a ship and sent down to Savannah so it would not have to travel through Northern territory. (Photograph by John Walker Guss.)

Hundreds of Confederate soldiers died defending the city and across many distant battlefields. Laurel Grove Cemetery set aside a section for these fallen Southern heroes and eventually maintained the largest number of Confederate graves of any cemetery in Savannah. One of the first to be interred was Col. Francis Bartow, 8th Georgia Regiment, the first Georgia officer to be killed in the Civil War. (Collection of John Walker Guss.)

Lt. Col. Charles Colcock Jones Jr. (1831–1893) was born in Savannah. A well-educated man, he was elected mayor of Savannah in 1859. On August 1, 1861, Jones enlisted in the Chatham Artillery. He was later put in charge of artillery for the Georgia district. During the siege, he commanded all of the artillery. After the war, Jones wrote a detailed book called *The Siege of Savannah*, which contained detailed information of the defenses around Savannah. He also wrote *A Historical Sketch of Tomochichi* in 1868. (Collection of the Coastal Heritage Society.)

Francis S. Bartow (1818–1861) was a native of Savannah. He was the first officer of Georgia killed at the First Battle of Manassas (known to Northerners as Bull Run). Before the war he declared, "I am tired of this endless controversy…If the storm is to come, and it seems to me as though it must, be its fury ever so great, I court it now in the day of vigor and strength." He became the colonel of the 8th Georgia Infantry and commanded a brigade at Manassas. As he was dying he told his men, "They have killed me boys, but never give up the field."

Francis S. Bartow was brought back to Savannah and laid to rest in Laurel Grove Cemetery where hundreds of brave Confederate soldiers would later join him. (Photograph by John Walker Guss.)

One of the great generals of the Confederate army was Lafayette McLaws (1821–1897). Like so many of the great leaders of the Civil War, he was a West Point graduate. He began his service with the Confederate army in Savannah assigned to Fort Pulaski, Thunderbolt Battery, and the Oglethorpe Barracks. McLaws later rose to the rank of major general in 1862 and served as a division commander in the First Corps under the command of Gen. James Longstreet. He fought in the major campaigns of the Army of Northern Virginia, including Gettysburg. Even though they had been boyhood friends, General Longstreet had McLaws relieved of command in 1863. He later returned Savannah to help defend the city against General Sherman. McLaws continued serving the Confederate cause until the final surrender at Bennett Farm in Durham, North Carolina. He returned to settle in Savannah.

Lafayette McLaws was respected by his men. He was a soldier's general. Some of the men he led throughout the war rest not far from his grave in the Confederate section in Laurel Grove, including the author's ancestor, Sgt. Jeremiah E. Johns, 50th Georgia Company A. McLaws's tombstone reads, "He knew when to lead us in, and he always brought us out." (*A Soldier's General: The Civil War Letters of Major General Lafayette McLaws* by John C. Oeffinger; photograph by John Walker Guss.)

Gen. Gilbert Sorrel Moxley grew up in Savannah. In 1861, he was serving as a clerk with the Central of Georgia Railroad. However, when his militia unit, the Georgia Hussars, was called up for duty, he began an illustrious military career first taking part in the seizure of Fort Pulaski. His unit was later garrisoned at Skidaway Island. Moxley was eager to "see the elephant" so he offered his services to Gen. James Longstreet, serving as his aide-de-camp throughout the war. Moxley returned home after the war and was a successful businessman. He is buried in the family mausoleum in Laurel Grove Cemetery. (Collection of the Coastal Heritage Society.)

George S. Groce (April 1835–January 12, 1862) was an officer serving in the Bartow Artillery. He was stationed at the defenses around Skidaway Island. Unfortunately, he would not last the war. (Collection of Fort James Jackson.)

The brothers Edward P. Postell and Chase B. Postell are buried on either side of their mother. This was all too common for both the North and the South. Maria Monroe Postell's two sons served in the 18th Georgia Battalion of the Confederacy. Edward P. Postell died at the age of 18 in the Siege of Fort Wagner and his brother Chase B. Postell, age 21, died at Sailors Creek on April 6, 1865. (Photograph by John Walker Guss.)

Eight

A New Age of Fortifications

A new age of fortifications was being built to defend the United States. A new threat arose when the sinking of the battleship *Maine* brought on the Spanish-American War. Afterward, the world exploded into a war involving all major powers. The advancement of new technology brought forth massive cannons, mechanized tanks, and the airplane. Never again would a fort—earthen, brick, or concrete—protect defenders. (Tybee Historical Society.)

In 1897, Fort Screven became part of the new system of fortifications in the United States, which became known as the Endicott system, named for Secretary of War William C. Endicott. The fort went through several names beginning with Fort Tybee, then Fort Graham, and finally Fort Screven in honor of Revolutionary War hero Brig. Gen. James Screven who is buried in Midway, Georgia. (Collection of the Tybee Historical Society and History of Fort Screven by James Mack Adams.)

The Savannah Volunteers continued service throughout World Wars I and II. They trained heavily on the artillery pieces mounted on the walls of Fort Screven. (Collection of the Savannah Volunteer Veterans.)

120

One of the first buildings a visitor sees upon entrance to the Fort Screven complex is the guardhouse. Here soldiers stand in formation preparing for guard duty. The guardhouse has been preserved. (Collection of the Tybee Historical Society.)

This is a great view of a 12-inch mortar being fired. The guns fired 700-pound shells, which were hurled in a high arc and dropped upon their target. This mortar served Battery Habersham. (Collection of the Tybee Historical Society.)

Battery Habersham was added to the fortifications of Fort Screven in 1898, one month after the Spanish American War ended. This battery was manned by 7 officers and 219 enlisted personnel. Here, an artillery crew at Battery Habersham just fired a 12-inch Mortar. (Collection of the Tybee Historical Society.)

Soldiers of Battery Brumby pose in this humorous photograph taken of the massive 8-inch disappearing gun. Although these men are enjoying a break in the action, they were very well trained and could man and fire this gun at a moments notice. This new type of artillery was mechanically raised to fire and then lowered for the crew to reload behind the safety of the concrete wall. (Collection of the Tybee Historical Society.)

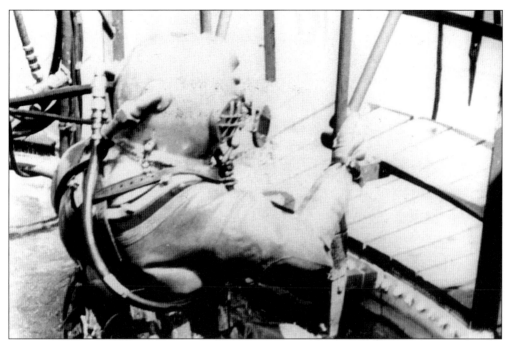

During World War II, Fort Screven opened the United States Army Engineer Diving and Salvage School to train military engineers in salvage and repair of bomb-damaged ports. Col. Charles B. Meyer initiated the program. The units of the 1051st, 1052nd, 1053rd, and 1054th Engineer Port Construction and Repair Groups in this specialized field served at Fort Screven. It became the only training facility of its type in the United States. (Collection of the Tybee Historical Society.)

Bands have always been a part of the military structure. They provide entertainment and boost morale among the ranks. These well-dressed soldiers are the men of the 14th Coast Artillery Corps Band stationed at Fort Screven. The photograph was taken in 1910. (Collection of the Tybee Historical Society.)

Fort Pulaski had been deemed obsolete at the beginning of the Civil War. To defend Cockspur Island and the entrance to the Savannah River, Battery Hambright was constructed on June 1, 1899. It was named in honor of Horace George Hambright, an officer who died in 1896 while serving in the North Dakota Territory. The battery had an armament of two 3-inch guns.

The author happened to be standing on the walls of Battery Hambright when he caught a rare glimpse of the Liberty ship *John Brown*, which actually served in World War II. On this day, it took some 500 guests on a cruise during Memorial Day weekend 2002 to experience a brief moment in history. Liberty ships were military transports used during World War II to carry troops, ammunition, weapons, food, and even prisoners of war. Savannah had shipyards that built Liberty ships that traveled down the river and overseas just as the *John Brown* is doing here. The *John Brown* is one of only two Liberty ships in existence. It is permanently docked in Baltimore, Maryland. (Photograph by John Walker Guss.)

The Savannah Volunteer Guard stand in formation in this 1910 photograph. They are dressed in their finest uniforms in front of their headquarters on Bull Street. Sadly as veterans passed away the organization was too small to maintain their home which had housed the unit for over one hundred years. The building was sold to the Savannah School of Art and Design, but has been restored and preserved. (Collection of the Savannah Volunteer Veterans.)

This was once the headquarters for the Savannah Volunteer Guard. Organized in 1802, this hometown unit saw military service through World War II. The headquarters is an elaborate structure with two impressive cannons guarding the entrance. It is said that these guns were buried during the Civil War to keep them out of the hands of the Union army. (Photograph by John Walker Guss.)

In 1941 terror struck the entire world when Adolf Hitler and his massive German war machine stormed through Europe and Russia. While the war raged, a small group of men met in this building on Bull Street in Savannah, Georgia. It had been the headquarters of the local military unit, the Chatham Artillery. It was in this very building that on January 28, 1942, the most famous air force in history would be formed. The Eighth Air Force would become the mightiest air force in the entire world, playing the most significant role in destroying the German aggressors. These "flying fortresses" were a new age of warfare and defense that forever changed the course of defending a nation. (Photographs by John Walker Guss.)

INDEX

Anderson, Maj. Edward C. (C.S.A.) 46
Anderson, Maj. George W. (C.S.A.) 97
Barton, Col. William B. (U.S.A.) 69
Bartow, Col. Francis S. (C.S.A.) 115
Battery Beaulieu 86, 88
Battery Bonaventure 61
Battery Brumby 122
Battery Daniels 88
Battery Habersham 121
Battery Hambright 124
Battery RoseDew 82, 86
Battery Stephens 87
Beauregard, Gen. P.G.T. (C.S.A.) 106
Boggs, Gen. William Robertson (C.S.A.) 79
Bourke, Thomas 34
Campbell, Lt. Col. Archibald 14–16, 19
Causton's Bluff (Fort Bartow) 81–83
Central of Georgia Railroad 23, 111
Coastal Heritage Society 59, 60
Confederate Monument 113
Christophe, King Henri 25
Crosby, William (C.S. Navy) 95
C.S.S. *Atlanta* Ironclad 90–92
C.S.S. *Georgia* Ironclad 93, 94
C.S.S. *Nashville* 100,101
C.S.S. *Savannah* Ironclad 92, 93
Dallas, Moses (C.S.A. Navy, Pilot) 95
Davis, President Jefferson 39
D'Estaing, Gen. Charles Henri 25
Duke of Argyle 10
Ebenezer, Fortifications 14, 16
Elbert, Gen. Samuel 26
Eighth Air Force 126
Eighth Georgia Regiment (C.S.A.) 114, 115
Evacuation of Savannah 108, 109
Ferguson, Dougald (Republican Blues) 98
Fifty-Fifth Massachusetts Regiment 50, 51
First Georgia Regulars 62

First Georgia Volunteers 40
Fort Argyle 10, 11
Fort Bartow (Causton's Bluff) 81–83
Fort Boggs 79-81
Fort Jackson 34–37, 44–49, 52–60, 73, 110
Fort Lawton 61
Fort Lee (Battery Lee) 73–78
Fort McAllister 86, 96–99, 102–105
Fort Morris 17, 18
Fort Prevost 24
Fort Pulaski 38, 43, 63–70
Fort Screven 119–123
Fort Tattnall 84
Fort Thunderbolt 84, 85
Fort Wayne 24
Fort Wimberly 88
Forty-Eighth New York Regiment 62, 68, 69, 71, 72
Fuser, Col. L.V. 18
Georgia Historical Commission 58
Gilmore, Gen. Quincy A. 63
Greene, Gen. Nathaniel 31
Groce, George S. (Bartow Artillery) 117
Hardee, Gen. William (C.S.A.) 106
Haitian Soldiers 23, 25
Hazen, Gen. William B. (U.S.A.) 102
Hessian of Welworth Regiment 16
Howe, Maj. Gen. Robert 19
Irish Jasper Greens Monument 42
Isle of Hope 88
Jackson, Col. James 27
Jasper, Sgt. William 28
Jefferson, President Thomas 21, 33
Jewish Cemetery 23
Jones, Lt. Col. Charles Colcock 114
Jones, Noble 12
Lawton, Gen. Alexander R. 61
Lafayette, Gen. Marquis de 32
Laurel Grove Cemetery 114

Lee, Gen. Robert E. 38, 45
Lighthouse, Tybee Island 44
Lighthouse, Cockspur Island 43
Lincoln, Gen. Benjamin 23, 26
Lincoln, President Abraham 39
Martello Tower 62
McCrady, Capt. John 97
McIntosh, Gen. Lachlan 20
McLaws, Maj. Gen. Lafayette 84, 116
McRee, Capt. William 35
Midway 30, 31
Mud Fort 21
Nutt, Lt. Col. William (55th Massachusetts) 50
Oglethorpe, Gen. James Edward 9, 10
Olmstead, Col. Charles H. 62
Pontoon Bridges 108
Postell, Chase B. (C.S.A. 18th GA. Batt.) 118
Postell, Edward P. (C.S.A. 18th Batt.) 118
Prevost, Gen. Augustine 18, 24
Pulaski, Gen. Casimir 29
Republican Blues 41, 42, 96, 98
Salter's Island 21
Salzburgers 14
Savannah, Riverfront 40, 108, 109
Savannah Volunteer Guard 41, 120
Screven, Brig. Gen. James 30, 31
Seventy-First Highland Regiment 16
Sherman, Gen. William Tecumseh (U.S.A.) 107, 112
Siege of Savannah 22, 23, 27
Sims, Pvt. Elbert C. (C.S.A. 7th GA. Cavalry) 98
Sorrel, Gen. Gilbert Moxley (C.S.A.) 117
Spring Hill Redoubt 23
Stewart, Brig. Gen. Daniel 30, 31
Sunbury 17
Savannah Shipyard 107
Third Rhode Island Heavy Artillery Regiment (U.S.A.) 70, 71
Tybee Island 44, 62
Tattnall, Commodore Josiah 89
Trotter, Second Lt. James Monroe (55th Massachusetts Regiment) 50
Twenty-Second Georgia Heavy Artillery 46
U.S.S. Montauk 101
U.S.S. Nahant 99
U.S.S. Passaic Ironclad 99
U.S.S. Patapsco Ironclad 99
U.S.S. Waterwitch 95
U.S.S. Weehawken Ironclad 91
Wayne, Gen. "Mad" Anthony 14, 20
Webb, Captain W.A. (C.S.S. Atlanta) 90
Willink, Jr., Henry F. 90
Wormsloe 12, 13